EAT OUT

RESTAURANT DESIGN AND FOOD EXPERIENCES

gestalten

PREFACE

A

Rohini Wahi

The INGREDIENTS

The RECIPE

From the Eucharist to Emily Post, ice cream cones to silver spoons, the act of eating has long been the source of elaborate human ritual. If man is, as they say, a social animal, then beyond its caloric function, eating, and eating out, is one of the most fundamental ways to satisfy the itch for interaction or to escape entirely from it, to reach outside ourselves, or to withdraw inward. Food and eating spaces give us the excuse to wrangle a deal, form an alliance, fall in love, and break up. Or they create sensual experiences that transport us to places that are outside ordinary experience even when they live inside our bodies.

On the following pages, the editors have made a selection of international food spaces, not based on the menu (though food design is an equally worthy topic) but structured instead around the character of the interior. These are designs that choreograph our consumption, whether it is eating, drinking, or shopping for food or drink. They represent an exploration of the relationship amongst our spaces, communities, and food; of the elements that determine the nature of an eating experience, and what is needed to foster an exceptional one. What sets one species of restaurant apart from another and why is this difference significant to restaurateurs, chefs, and patrons, alike?

These restaurants, bars, cafes, supermarkets, food trucks, art installations, and one table in the sky fall into nine categories that suggest what it is that people value explicitly or viscerally about the spaces in which they choose to eat, about the businesses that feed them, and about what keeps them coming back for seconds. They represent a celebration of this uniquely intimate, obscene, satisfying, and human rite: the diner swallows food and the dining room swallows the diner.

Amplifying all the design elements in support of an already amped-up menu (sweets, frozen yogurt, coffee, or fast food), pop interiors work, perhaps in a small part, to gloss over the sinfulness of the indulgence. Even more, however, they serve to make the experience and, not leastly, the brand feel larger than life. Especially appealing to families with children or adults looking for a thrill, this bigness suggests a game, something whimsical, naughty, or both. As in times past, inexpensive food and loud design enjoy a close connection. At its worst, this can be vulgar; at its best, invigorating, even intoxicating.

So it is with *Solid Air's* TOKYO BAR in Manhattan, which is defined by the manga-like comic frames that cover the ceiling and parts of the walls. Colored neon lights outline each character's talking bubble to create an effect that is part playful and part red-light district. On the other hand, *Asylum's* Singapore-based FROLICK yogurt shops are wallpapered with colorful panels on which saucy slogans related to the frozen treat read: "We stay hard longer," "Size does matter," and "I like it topless" in large type.

In recent years, a number of franchises like FROLICK have been making an effort to vary their interior concepts according to location. McDonalds and Starbucks, leaders of global retail imperialism have even begun opening unbranded spaces or, phrased another way, spaces that are designed to appeal to locals (wherever those locals may be on the planet) instead of to the company's CEO and marketing divisions. Fast food restaurants and coffeehouses, however, aren't the only ones to expand into chains today: Even innovators and higher brow establishments like PONTUS! in Sweden are proliferating; using the same name while experimenting with the character of the interiors. Aside from the downtown location with its exclamation mark for emphasis, the Pontus group consists of Pontus by the Sea, From Pontus – Gourmet to Go and a hotel (one assumes it has a restaurant) "by Pontus." To the great delight of Malmo locals, the quantity hasn't diluted the quality one smidgeon.

Even artist *Tobias Rehberger* has gotten in on the chain expansion. The artist, who won a Golden Lion for his Italian pavilion bar at the Venice Biennale,

"franchised" his design by creating a second installment at another culturally exalted institution, the Kunsthalle in Basel, Switzerland. Rehberger based his designs on the dazzle graphics of First World War battleships, which were dressed in stunning (literally) op art-like patterns to confuse the enemy's read on the ship's position, speed, and direction. In both cafés, Rehberger punctuated relentless black and white stripes and chevrons, which covered every surface of the space in every which way, with neon colors. These are perhaps apotheoses of the graphic interior aesthetic, which imposes a visual experience based on large-scale (room-sized) illustration and pattern. These can be intense enough, like Rehberger's, to radically exaggerate or even delightfully overpower the menu or, if the food is extreme enough, to serve as an extension of it. The importance here is placed on the engagement of the diner, whether he has an epileptic seizure, feels slightly dizzy, or walks out feeling euphorically caffeinated. In the case of visitors to the Venice Biennale, one assumes that caffeination would have been entirely welcome.

Another species of eating spot that may feel almost as dynamic, invokes the high-tech in its visuals (menus projected onto the tabletop), or in its construction (using algorithmic software or computer numerically controlled routers). BANQ in Boston is clad in swagging, staggered, CNC-milled layers of wood, for instance. But these restaurants can suggest as much about the low-tech, the natural, and the handcrafted as they do about technology; references that bring us around again to the qualities that make up the finest food: low-tech, natural ingredients, made by mom.

In FLOOD, *Mathieu Lehanneur* creates a space that is genuinely way ahead of its time (making furniture that filters, measures, and indicates air quality to match the purity of the food being served), but he harnesses something primitive (algae) to do it. In Hong Kong's PISSARRO bistro, *Michael Young* CNC-milled the front door and digitized an impressionist painting, on the one hand, but then hand-blew his own lighting fixtures in a workshop at the foot of Mt. Fuji and hung thousands of pieces of hand-folded paper on the wall, each a pixel in a section of the digitized Pissarro canvas.

Like Young, designers everywhere are coming up with a more flexible and inclusive vision of grandeur. At a juncture in history when more people have more than ever before, we must redefine the notion of luxury. If it is more widespread, how do we create a new standard by which to organize the social ladder? In restaurant interiors, the definition of grand has become more about culture than caste, more about authenticity (of ingredients and of materials) than artifice, more focused on health than hedonism.

A

So, forget the velvet rope. Exclusivity is the province of those in the know: if you can find the deliberately mismarked APOTHEKE in a dark alley off the Bowery in New York's Chinatown, you can take the cure in this 18th-century apothecary: "Prescriptions Served Daily," the menu reads, listing unique cocktails under the categories Health & Beauty, Pharmaceuticals, House Remedies or Therapeutic Treatments, and featuring unusual ingredients like absinthe, opium, and "cocoa" leaves (not to be confused with coca, one wonders?). In Stockholm, OPERAKALLEREN'S historical interior was renovated opulently by *Claesson Koivisto Rune.* The designers highlighted the authenticity of the original finishes precisely by using exceedingly new materials: in the dining room, large mirrors (a classic symbol of grandiosity) were tinted gold instead of silver and laminated with a new lenticular film that blurs reflections at certain angles while directing the gaze of diners to the decadently carved ceiling, which remains in sharp focus overhead.

In both grand and private spaces, the social aspect of eating becomes paramount. At the communal table, in a more intimate setting, guests sit beside friends deliberately, and strangers, who are seated beside them by the host, incidentally. At the chef's table, the communal experience is raised a notch, with the added feeling of proximity to an open kitchen, to the preparation of the food, and to those preparing it. This bestows the privilege of being "involved" in this creative, behind-the-scenes action. The private dining room is booked by a group looking to do a little business or bonding or both, en masse. These rooms have become popular again, but with a more restrained showiness, not in honor of the sagging world economy (although, granted, conspicuous consumption has dropped conspicuously out of favor); rather due to a renewed focus on eating good food in good company and attending to the brisk business of being a social (and professional) animal. In these chambers, with their subdued silks and limited gold accents, the construction and maintenance of relationships is the special of the day: *Project Orange* designed a dining room in the WHITECHAPEL GALLERY, where art collectors and gallerists can hammer out their high-stakes financial and cultural alliances. At CONDUIT in San Francisco, the private becomes public: *Natoma Architects* exposed the "private" dining room behind glass walls, formalizing the separation between the plebeians and the cloistered guests, who are presented like a precious artifact in a museum box.

Beside grand interiors, straightforward eateries feel like the emperor without his clothes. But they wear their asceticism with pride; after all, frank spaces serve "honest" food. And don't mistake a straightforward space for a dully pragmatic one. These eateries are functionally practical, replacing our attention on the senses: taste, smell, touch, color and the clattering of saucepans from the kitchen.

The purpose of the visual restraint? To keep guests attuned to the sensations of eating by keeping the volume low on the interior design. (A restaurant like Frankfurt's MICRO FINE DINING by *3Deluxe,* with a pervasive design that nonetheless allows diners to cocoon themselves in their own dining "pockets" via long tendrils that hang from the ceiling, is the exception rather than the rule in this context.) Even as the straightforward dining room eschews pretension and gimmicks in favor of candor and comfort, it is often no less extraordinary in its appearance. After all, chicken soup still looks delicious.

Tokyo's ORI HIGAYASHI gift shop sells traditional sweets and gifts and shows shoppers how to best present them. Designed by the aptly named *Simplicity,* it is a box, glazed floor-to-ceiling, that seems to have been captured in a color photograph; a perfectly spare composition in rice paper and bare wood that is the picture of austere refinement. At the other extreme, in Syracuse, Italy, *Francesco Moncada* built PIZZA PEREZ from materials typically piled in the corner of a construction site – fiberglass, shipyard plywood – that he left unvarnished and unembellished. Like the pizza on the menu, the ingredients were good, the construction was superbly done: the lack of finishes became irrelevant.

This interest in the unembellished has grown among food space designers today. In contrast to the 1990s' glamour-driven and unabashedly trendy emphasis on places to see and be seen, the naughts have witnessed a clear movement toward emphasizing the quality, provenance, and authenticity of food while expressing this in our food space. In some part, this parallels our growing concern over environmental crises and issues of sustainability and responsible living, but the rustic chic approach is not limited to this. The embrace of elegant rawness is anchored in our trust and memory of familiar (or historically "familiar") objects. It has become a search for authenticity of experience as much as the purity of food. Therefore, it entails a respect for the small, local, family-run places (the farm and the farmer's market, the village butcher shop and the milkman) that once grew, produced, and distributed our food on a scale that we could relate to. It also honors an era when we not only knew where our food came from; we knew precisely where the people who made it came from. The focus on real relationships and responsible eating and living is literally built into the interior of Cape Town's BIRDS BOUTIQUE CAFÉ by *Frauke Stegmann.* The resourcefulness of Birds' construction – from materials collected at the local hardware store and held together in places with rip-ties – reflects the hard, humble labor that went into the growing and production of the food on offer.

Projects like Birds are labors of love. Aside from the deep-pocket restaurant brands, there has been a profusion of small, personal, passion-driven projects in the form of curated food outlets like

HEARTSCHALLENGER, which sells sweets and other somewhat random products from a fleet of diminutive pink trucks. There are cupcake joints and third wave coffee culture outlets run by that one person who wants to – and can! and does! – make the best coffee or cupcakes in town.

Some engagingly eclectic projects exhibit the same passion: Copenhagen's KARRIERE restaurant juxtaposes design and art, taking both out of the fussy gallery and bringing them into the food space. The result is an interior that improvises a multitude of extraordinary individual moments as guests listen and spy through peepholes between terrace tables or watch, charmed, as a functionally upside-down sink (an artwork called Fountain) shoots water from its drain over the faucet. Personal projects create personal dining experiences.

Finally, to create the truly unexpected eating experiences, there are the "performers," chefs and designers and restaurateurs who take the idea of the food event further. These spaces and happenings become immersive: In London, *Bompas & Parr* filled a room with the vapors of gin & tonic which visitors imbibed through their eyeballs. At PROEF, culturally critical product designer *Marije Vogelzang* asks if we taste differently when the food is at a different temperature than expected, or if potato crisps would still be enjoyable if they sounded like jelly. By choreographing eating events and letting serendipity take over during the meal, Vogelzang questions long and deeply held conventions. *Martí Guixé's* FOOD FACILITY was a temporary restaurant that turned the mechanism of Boolean online searches into an interior: diners ordered take-out from other restaurants and ate it in FOOD FACILITY, splitting orders with other guests if they wanted to have a Thai appetizer, Surinamese main course, and an Italian dessert in a single meal. *Martijn Engelbregt's* REST. was a pile of 45 stacked picnic tables. Guests went on "adventure hikes" to harvest edible weeds while staff collected scraps that would have been tossed out by other local eateries. Then the chef turned these odds and ends into artful meals like blackberry-muesli puree garnished with edible wildflowers. These installations, performances, and meals appeal to basic human instincts. They also renew our relationship to food and culture, which means of course, to ourselves. Ask yourself: when was the last time you tasted something for the very first time?

by
SHONQUIS
MORENO

POP

01

The pop aesthetic is one that makes beauty out of the banal and finds it in both exaggeration and repetition. It is the opposite of subtlety and all about the robust, the brilliant, even the overwhelming. Appealing to a younger audience, and to families and kids, designers are using bright neon colors and hypnotic patterns, exuberant wall murals and illustration, even walls that reach into the room to create an

immersive experience that can range from playful and friendly to ironic and even pushy. Walls, no longer a 2D architectural element, are given depth: chocolate drips from the ceiling of Wonderwall's GODIVA SHOP, yogurt melts into the SNOG shops by ico design and Cinimod Studio. This voluptuous extrusion is matched by elaborate lighting, behind the walls or overhead, using hues from cool violet or orange

to shades that shift through time of day and season. Robust texture is no less a tool of the pop mentality: designers may weave a "textile" from a profusion of 3D patterns clustered frenetically against the wall or dripping in long cylindrical pendants from the ceiling. This delirious layering creates a complex eye-level landscape that makes the interior dynamic. Although pop, with its eye-candy and 80s references, is a democratic aesthetic, characterizing international, consumer-coddling, unpretentious businesses, their looks can sometimes prove more delicious than the smells of the food coming from their kitchens. Skewing the scale of objects or images – making them smaller or larger than expected – can make an entire brand, not just an interior or the objects in it, larger than life.

TJEP.
Praq, 2008, Amersfoort / the Netherlands

Project Team : **Frank Tjepkema, Janneke Hooymans, Tina Stieger, Leonie Janssen, Bertrand Gravier, Camille Cortet**

This restaurant is designed to welcome families without looking like a (kids') playground. Second in the *Praq* franchise, the Amersfoort location features a monumental farm-style roof composed of massive wooden beams. As for the rest, it resembles a larger-than-life dollhouse that confuses furniture with toys without leaning on clichés: a table becomes a window, a bus, or a kitchen. The six-meter-high partition in the center of the room looks like an abstracted cloud, evoking something of a colorful game while providing clean, geometric forms that contrast well with the rustic structure. One space is reserved for children and their parents while another, a slightly cozier and more sophisticated Toyland, is reserved for adults.

VONSUNG / PODIUM

Kids Cafe Piccolo,
2009, Seoul / Korea

Client : **Kids Cafe Piccolo**

London-based studio VONSUNG collaborated with Podium to art direct, name, brand, and design the print, collateral, packaging, uniforms, way-finding; and a website for this highbrow kids' café and then applied many of its solutions to the interior of the café, itself. In this inaugural flagship café for children – which includes a playground, playroom, party room, and a library – VONSUNG challenged the preconceived uses of its graphic design elements, turning them into idiosyncratic interior statements. The identity of the café was created using Roman alphabet characters to make learning more enjoyable and interactive. The interior features traditional decorative finishing products that have been used unconventionally to make quirky features that complement the modern and interactive cafés for adults that abound in Seoul. In the spacious play area, lengths of soft timber floor planks were used at perpendicular angles across one wall to create a series of rectangles and squares, reminiscent of a tree house. The walls were then painted a cool pastel color to complement the flooring and bright furnishings. In the party room, a corbel – a decorative architectural support – was used as a floating shelf without the usual brackets and visible fixings. It is a design that incorporates the inventiveness and fresh view of objects that marks childhood and turns this into a space that will, in turn, no doubt encourage inventiveness and a fresh view of things.

ICO DESIGN & CINIMOD STUDIO

Snog Pure Frozen Yogurt,
2008, London / UK

Account Manager : **Sandra Dartnell** | Creative Director : **Ben Tomlinson** |
Design : **Amanda Gaskin** | Illustrator : **Akira Chatani** |
Photography : **Fernando Manoso**

Inspired by the need to make a warm and inviting space to counteract London's damp and chilly climate, which is decidedly not conducive to the consumption of frozen treats, the designers created a deliberately quirky, but inviting environment. A moving ceiling, a fascia with fins, and a Martian flower garden are just a few of the design features that greet *Snog* customers. The shops are a joint project between ico, Studio Uribe, and Dominic Harris from Cinimod Studio, envisaged as a social destination based on a retail concept the teams dubbed "The Eternal Summer." This theme led them to envision a warm, bright environment with a photographic grass floor and mushroom-shaped tables where customers leave with smiles, and perhaps a little frozen yogurt stuck to their faces.

Snog South Kensington

Snog Soho

ASYLUM
Frolick, 2008, Singapore

Client : **Frolick** | *Creative Direction* : **Chris Lee** | *Design* : **Edwin Tan** |
Photography : **Edwin Tan (Lumina Photography)**

Multidisciplinary creative agency, Asylum, wanted to approach the interiors of this yogurt shop in an unexpected way, rather than follow the conventional health-conscious image that other brands push. An immaculate white café-like interior is lined on one wall with tall, layered graphic panels papered with blown up words and cheerful colors. To give *Frolick* a politically incorrect attitude, the storefront is dotted with badges that sport naughty slogans like "We stay hard longer," "Size does matter," and "I like it topless." The badges are given away so that customers may keep them as collectibles and look forward to updated ones with each new store opening.

[A]

[A] Frolick — Serangoon Gardens : The designers used a recurring theme, creating buttons that give customers a take-out that won't melt and at the same time add a slight variation to the interior design, keeping it fresh.
[B] Frolick — Millenia Walk : Frolick's third outlet was its first in a mall. The company intended this to be a take-out kiosk with minimal complimentary seating.
[C] Frolick — Holland Village : Frolick's first (flagship) store in a busy eating area. The designers sought to create an eye-catching outlet that is loud and unique among dessert cafés.
[D] Frolick — Tampines One : Frolick's second mall outlet placed greater emphasis on the sit-in experience. At the same time, they worked to maintain the ease of take-out by placing the counter near the entrance.

[B]

[C]

[D]

BUDI PRADONO
blu apple Frozen Yogurt Café,
2009, Jakarta / Indonesia

Client: **Blu Apple** | Project Architect: **Budi Pradono** |
Assistant project architects: **Yuli Sri Hartanto, Rina Nur Aisah** |
Design Supervisors: **Budi Pradono, Yuli Sri Hartanto, Rina Nur Aisah,
Ian Flood** | Graphic Design: **Ahmett Salina** | Contractor: **PT. KANG,
Rukamto Laksana** | Project Manager: **Yohanes Sembiring** |
Site Supervisor: **Indra Sukmana** | Workshop Supervisor: **Sukandar** |
Signage Specialist: **Rhino advertising, Aming** | Sofa Specialist: **PT. KANG.**

Because frozen yogurt outlets are now ubiquitous in malls, the designer's challenge lay in creating novelty: of products, serving methods, logo, image, and architecture. The company helped this effort by serving its yogurt on hot pancakes topped with more than 30 types of fruit and sold self-served (with price determined by weight). To appeal to the product's local target market, graphics created by Ahmett Salina feature an apple logo in silhouette surrounded by colorful fireflies. At the Semanggi Mall, the spaces to the left and right of the café are quite dim, demanding that the interior palette be assertive but calm enough to highlight the colorful logo and fruit. Above the white epoxy floor, ice chunks float in the air and melt downwards so that customers can serve themselves from the ends of these dripping chunks.

STUDIO GAIA
Aroma Espresso Bar,
2009, New York / USA

Client : **Aroma Espresso Bar** | Photography : **Moon Lee**

When the Israeli café chain *Aroma Espresso Bar* opened its second New York location on Manhattan's Upper West Side, they again commissioned local Studio GAIA to design the interior – it was just the interior they wanted to be different. With vivid colors, playful wall graphics, and fashionable chairs that encourage loitering, the two-story coffeehouse translates the concept for the company's original New York venue—a long, narrow space in Soho with a huge window facade—to a different, more family-oriented and kid-friendly neighborhood. In the new bar, red wall tiles arch down from the ceiling to create a modern-yet-domestic ambiance, as if it were a kitchen at home. The distinctive rhythmic arches, separated by niches that contain indirect lighting, give the space a dynamic, theatrical look, while also visually caffeinating a dull, pedestrian stretch of 72nd Street. The firm has also designed a third Manhattan Aroma location, which will open in the Financial District, where a more muted material palette and earth-toned color scheme are in keeping with a buttoned-down Wall Street clientele.

IPPOLITO FLEITZ GROUP
WakuWaku, 2008,
Hamburg / Germany

Client : **WakuWaku Restaurants GmbH** |
Photography : **Zooey Braun**

"Waku" is Japanese and means stir-fried, cooked hot, and at the same time exciting and tantalizing. *WakuWaku's* culinary approach is based on performance, allowing guests to watch the cooks at work. All dishes are wok-based and use only organic ingredients. The wok cooking makes it possible to prepare individual dishes in under 5 minutes while retaining the nutrients and aroma of the ingredients, despite using only a small amount of oil. The menu is also unconventional, offering classic Asian dishes alongside German culinary classics such as Currywurst and Tafelspitz. The opening of the first branch of the restaurant chain *WakuWaku* in Hamburg's city center, trumpets the company's self-proclaimed revolution of the fast food sector. *WakuWaku's* philosophy revolves around the concepts of sustainability, good value, and healthy food prepared fast. IFG

articulates this sustainability theme in the space in an undogmatic, creative, and unconventional way, from installing energy-efficient kitchen technology to fashioning the staff uniform from FAIR-TRADE-certified materials. On entering the restaurant, the customer first encounters the narrow end of this 17-meter-long box. A glass roof in the rear illuminates the interior, which is divided into two zones: the dining room and the service area that combines an order counter, kitchen, and takeout window into a single box, which is painted a strong shade of violet, *WakuWaku's* corporate color. The dining room features a floor-to-ceiling wooden bench that provides seating, a planter box, and an artist's gallery down the entire length of the room. The uniformity of the bench is interrupted by a variety of vintage wooden chairs, lacquered halfway up their legs, which are supplemented with a swinging loveseat and an unusual booth, which is simply an incision made through the wall in the negative shape of two benches facing each other. The colorful, lacquered surfaces at the base of chairs or on the wooden spoons that customers are given with their order number on it, form a dynamic contrast to expanses of stainless steel, plain white ceramic tile, and floor tiles in a randomized pattern of gray shades.

AB ROGERS
Little Chef, 2008,
Popham / UK

Client : **Little Chef / Heston Blumenthal** | Creative Direction, Design :
Ab Rogers Design | Branding, Graphics : **Praline** | Sound & Interactive Design :
Dominic Robson of 'Robson & Jones' | Photography : **John Short**

Michelin star-chef Heston Blumenthal and
Little Chef commissioned Ab Rogers Design to
create a new flagship for the franchise. Rogers
overhauled the *Little Chef* brand, from interior
design to graphics, menu and uniform, signage
and packaging. The team sifted through the history of the company, of US diners, British road-
side eating, from the days of horses and carts and
chophouses, eel and pie shops and butchers, to
create a design language informed by the past
but looking to the future. The materials they
chose are tough and energizing: tiles are hygienic
and durable while conveying a British sensibility; laminate and vinyl fabric communicate a synthetic modernity, 1950s diner nostalgia, vivid
color, and ease of maintenance. Because ceiling
tiles are usually dull, they printed a trompe l'oeil
sky on them. The kitchen became a strong focal
point when the designers created a bar that peels
from the tiled floor and serves as a frame for this
hub of frenetic (and entertaining) activity. Looking for a way to engage "the stop-and-pee bri-
gade," the Rogers team piped the sounds of a
restaurant kitchen – a symphony of crashing
pots and pans, sizzling fryers, and shouting
cooks – into the bathroom. As each visitor enters
the toilets, an interactive food-related sound or
song also plays, with Spike Milligan singing
about jelly or Morecambe and Wise telling jokes
about apples. The interior preserves the use of
the color red, which has always been associated
with the brand, but was expanded through the
full spectrum, from pink to orange through
bright red. They also introduced blues to echo
the sky and complement the red. All in all, the
restaurant has a sense of modernity that draws
on and appreciates the past.

WONDERWALL INC.

GODIVA Chocoiste Harajuku,
2009, Tokyo / Japan

Photography: **Kozo Takayama**

The theme of Godiva's new Tokyo flagship store was, unsurprisingly: "Treat thyself." Also unsurprisingly, Wonderwall was able to make this rather ordinary theme quite extraordinary while retaining the elegance of the brand. The shop features humorous but handsome design details, such as a melting chocolate ceiling, that the designers then combined with a primarily classical interior design.

MARION + MERCHE
Happy Pills, 2007,
Barcelona / Spain

MM dreamed up the product concept, creative strategy, and interior design of the *Happy Pills* sweet shop. Setting up their confectionary in the narrowest venue imaginable, beside Barcelona's Cathedral Square and sandwiched between two looming edifices, the designers found themselves in a neighborhood with few children but busloads of tourists and a handful of grumpy natives. To sell candy to this crowd, MM decided they needed to make the product entertaining for adults. "We came up with the fact, more or less proven by all, that eating something sweet engenders a slight improvement in mood," says one designer. "In this light, sweets are small mouthfuls of happiness. And today mouthfuls of happiness are most necessary for such serious setbacks as Sundays with no football, Mondays, and global warming." The sweets had to be a remedy against the ills of our time. Hence the name: *Happy Pills*. When it came time to put the idea into practice, the designers thought it best to endow the shop with a healthy and hygienic pharmaceutical aura, using clear vials and cheerful clean graphics that most people associate with aspirin or vitamin supplements. Customers fill a vial up with their preferred "remedies" and choose the label that best suits their mood. In Spanish or in English.

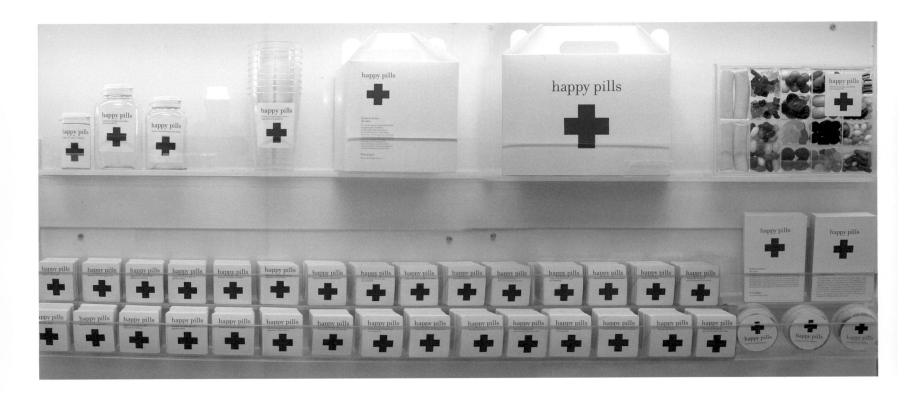

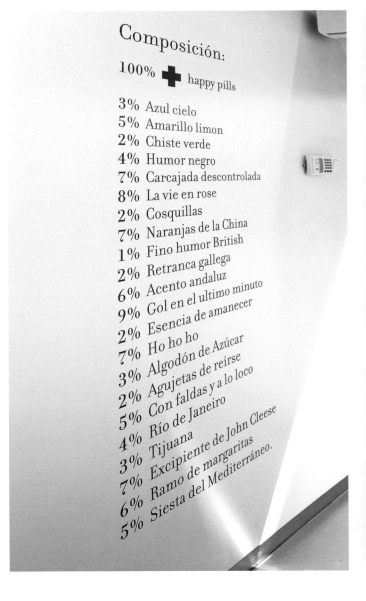

Composición:

100% ✚ happy pills

3% Azul cielo
5% Amarillo limon
2% Chiste verde
4% Humor negro
7% Carcajada descontrolada
8% La vie en rose
2% Cosquillas
7% Naranjas de la China
1% Fino humor British
2% Retranca gallega
6% Acento andaluz
9% Gol en el ultimo minuto
2% Esencia de amanecer
7% Ho ho ho
3% Algodón de Azúcar
2% Agujetas de reírse
5% Con faldas y a lo loco
4% Río de Janeiro
3% Tijuana
7% Excipiente de John Cleese
6% Ramo de margaritas
5% Siesta del Mediterráneo.

TOM DIXON WITH MIND DESIGN

Paramount, 2008,
London / UK

Client : **Paramount** | Interior Design : **Tom Dixon /
Design Research Studio** | Photography : **Mark Whitfield, Ed Reeve**

The design of an elite new members' club in London was inspired largely by the brutalist skyscraper in which it is situated. Crowning the top three floors of the 33-story Centre Point building by Richard Seifert, which on its completion in 1967 was one of the first skyscrapers in the city, the interiors borrow strategically from the distinctive geometric architectural elements with which the edifice is tattooed. Dixon molded the bar and other furnishings from the oversized mineral facets which have been such stars of his toolkit in recent years. Mind Design wed the building's brutalist geometry to a 1960s op art aesthetic (influenced by the work of French artist Victor Vasarely, whose optical images contributed to the eye-trumping look of 60's and 70's fashion, computer science, and architecture; the irony, in this application, being that his motto was "Art For All"). They built a series of four patterns, with each pattern made from a simple shape (hexagon, triangle, circle, and stripe) that was plucked from the building or its interior, and repeated 33 times (to represent each of the 33 floors). Variations on these motifs were applied to the club's brochures, stationery, menus, tapestry, signage, sliding glass screens, and more. Dixon and the client sought to stack and mass the geometric elements in such a way that each furniture or interior architectural element would look different while having a hectic coherence, as well as being elegant enough to suit the club atmosphere but at the same time remain true to the raw aesthetics of the building.

STUDIO LINSE
Café Chocolat Schiphol Airport, 2009, Amsterdam / the Netherlands

Client : **HMS Host services** |Design : **Yuhkichi Kawai** |
Photography : **Went&Navarro**

    Amsterdam-based Studio Linse, founded by Paul Alexander Linse, works on the conviction that design should communicate its purpose. To translate what the firm calls "the seductive chocolate experience" into expressive, sensual retail and café spaces in a highly exposed airport location, the designers took a "feminine" approach, which was suggested by the "soft touch" of chocolate. The interior features organic shapes and a strong decorative pattern that echoes the lace-like paper cup used to contain the original patisserie. A purple ribbon overhanging the café resembles the ribbon that wraps the company's confection boxes, and ties the space into the neighboring Bubbles Seafood & Wine Bar, while creating intimacy in a seating area that would otherwise have been transparently open to the vast airport terminal. Chocolat respects the airport building logistics by balancing this openness with a cozy retreat from the rush and crush of its highly trafficked location.

HOSOYA SCHAEFER ARCHITECTS

AnAn Restaurant,
2005 – 2007,
Wolfsburg / Germany

Client : **Autostadt GmbH, Wolfsburg, Germany |**
Design : **Hiromi Hosoya + Markus Schaefer, Hosoya Schaefer**
Architects, Zurich | CI : **Büro Destruct, Bern |**
Furniture : **Hosoya Schaefer Architects in collaboration with**
Quinze & Milan | Photography : **Iwan Baan**

AnAn is a Japanese noodle bar designed for Autostadt, Germany, the theme park and communications platform of the Volkswagen Group. HSA was asked to build a space that would represent contemporary Tokyo in microcosm. The geometric structure of the interior consists of a series of distorted hexagonal cells across floor and ceiling. This pattern is also used for some tables, vending machines, a coat room, plastic plates, and as a three-dimensional menu column. The cells are made of 25-mm-thick acrylic panels that reach 3.5 meters from floor to ceiling and are covered with graphics. The skewed grid in the floor is expressed as aluminum lines in the white polyurethane floor, and in the ceiling as light strips that illuminate the restaurant. An algorithm was developed that runs as a Maya plug-in to minimize the number of angles and radii for the fabrication of the various panels. The space is conceived to be both transparent and filled with extroverted graphics to create a heterogeneous, urban setting.

STUDIO GAIA

Sakae and Escoffier Restaurants – Busan Paradise Hotel, 2007, Busan / Korea

New York-based Studio GAIA redesigned this Korean hotel to include two restaurants. The character of the first, a Japanese eatery called *Sakae,* is a balance of opposites. Of its three distinct spaces, the most striking resembles the interior of a traditional Japanese gift box, its ceiling and one wall wrapped in scarlet kimono fabric that is threaded with cherry blossoms and, like a garment, arcs between wall and ceiling instead of forming a hard-angled corner. Counterpoint to the luxuriant old school textile that has been used, this radiused edge, pocket lighting, and bare stone flooring in clean lines evoke a sense of comfortable modernity. The old versus new theme of the interior design also reflects the pairing of hot and cold on the menu, as well as the nature of the climate outside: the powerful summer sun is relieved by a cool breeze that can be felt in waterfront seating that hems one wall of the restaurant.

A Chinese buffet restaurant called *Escoffier* is an extension of the lobby (also designed by GAIA), in which the emphasis is on a grand food display. In the main dining area, banquettes embraced by a curving envelope of dark wood are interspersed throughout the regular tables and chairs. Boxcar-sized spaces flank the dining room, also lined in dark wood with walls incised with a grid of dots or long vertical cuts that are backlit serenely with violet light.

SHH
ARCHITECTS
Teaspoon, 2008,
St. Petersburg / Russia

Client : **Teaspoon** | Design : **Neil Hogan,
Helen Hughes, Daniel de Groot**

SHH's concept for this 70-unit Russian tea room and pancake house franchise debuted in the form of a new 300-square-meter space in a St. Petersburg hypermarket. The interior features various seating zones, dramatic lighting, and an eye-catching 6-meter high wraparound ceramic wall, custom-designed by SHH. The designers were inspired by Russian folkloric art to create this black, white, and orange tile pattern, which was then accessorized with heavy cylindrical pendant lights with black exteriors and orange interiors, casting a warm light on the white furnishings below. It is a SHH design that speaks loudly.

GIANT DESIGN
Mad Mex, 2008,
Sydney / Australia

Client: **Mad Mex Pty Ltd** | Design: **Giant Design /**
Ed Kenny, Christopher Wilks | Graphics: **Holy Cow** |
Photography: **Andrew Worssam**

This 70-square-meter Mexican restaurant was infused with the flavors of Mexico without resorting to the sombreros and cactus clichés usually associated with Tex-Mex food. "We wanted to create a sexy urban space that is earthy and moody with lots of warmth and texture, and a little bit of grit," says Giant principal Ed Kenny. All the finishes, concrete breeze blocks, recycled timber, polished plasterwork, and a rust finish evoke the Central American country and the outdoor lifestyle that its climate affords. Kenny used stools fashioned from rescued road signs and remade by Trent Jansen, as well as a custom-made Corona chandelier (inspired by a Coke bottle fitting seen in Mexico City) to capture the beauty of Mexican resourcefulness and improvi-sation and its tools, the found object and all things homemade. Kenny translated the Mad Mex wrestler identity (created by Holy Cow!) into a tiled wall mural that articulates the brand ethos and concept. By keeping the open kitchen dark, the designer placed the greatest focus on the food. Where it should be.

KARIM RASHID
Switch, 2009, Dubai /
United Arab Emirates

Client: **Al–Bassam Group** | Photography: **Karim Rashid**

Dubai Mall's *Switch* restaurant features a strong, symmetrical interior wrapped by a continuous, undulating wall that carries much of the venue's seating. New York-based Karim Rashid's textural design, which provides a background for the play of light and shadow, evokes the dunes of the city's ever-encroaching desert. "I wanted to create an oasis free from chaos," Rashid explains. The space comprises a long rectangular shoebox partitioned into three sections, for dining, bar, and lounge, with stylized and backlit Arabic phrases serving as artwork against the ceiling. Long banquette seating in the dining room is intended to feel communal and reflect the teeming global culture that makes the city of Dubai unique. Rashid designed the banquette, lounge furniture, dining tables, and wall panels and had them manufactured locally. The buxom panels and bold use of glass and chrome give *Switch* a high gloss, cosmopolitan feel. Rashid's signature "digipop" patterns and scrolling LED text break

up these shiny, voluptuous surfaces; the designer kept the color scheme relatively low-key in order to better reflect the changing hue of the walls: throughout the day, the restaurant shifts from pink to purple to blue, and through green, yellow and red.

JAKOB SCHLAEPFER
Ruckstuhl Cafeteria, 2008,
Langenthal / Switzerland

Wallcovering Glinka by : **Jakob Schlaepfer** | Creative Director : **Martin Leuthold**

Swiss firm Jakob Schlaepfer usually weaves exquisite textiles for haute couture and prêt-a-porter fashion houses. Last spring it dressed the walls of the *Ruckstuhl Cafeteria* with a new wall, floor and ceiling textile called Glinka. Glinka features a foil fabric printed with more than 40 images (flowers, berries, fleurs-de-lys motifs, and a surreal combination of illustrative graphics and photographic realism) and bonded with a holographic film to produce a resilient sheet that can either be mounted directly on the wall as a wallcovering, or sandwiched between glass and used as a laminate for floors and ceilings. Whether seen in artificial or natural light, the blending of ornament, high-gloss reflection, and the holographic effect makes for high drama that is a sophisticated mix of Dior frock and Josef Franck graphics. Along with their patrons, today's fashionable restaurants must also dress for dinner.

SOLID AIR DESIGN

Tokyo Bar, 2007,
New York / USA

Client : **Transit General Office** | Design : **Yukiko Krigh and Mathias Krigh** | Photography : **Gion 2007**

"We wanted the space to breathe sex," says Solid Air co-principal Mathias Krigh. He and partner Yukiko Krigh imbued the small comfort food restaurant *Tokyo Bar,* in New York's decidedly unclaustrophobic loft-lined Tribeca, with the labyrinthine feeling of Tokyo's tiny neon-scribbled alleyways and hidden hot sheet hotels. The design was also inspired by the photography of Kishin Shinoyama (women in various stages of undress), Ridley Scott's dystopian 1980s film Blade Runner and Japanese artist, Taihei Shii, who created canvases literally lined with the spines of books. It seems like the images from these books have escaped to adorn the walls of the bar, which are slathered with manga-like anime frames (made in collaboration with four illustrators from Mashcomix) and neon-limned talking bubbles. Solid Air emphasized the Japanese characters and words, giving depth to the manga, which seems to swell from the 2D walls into three dimensions. On the curb, a projection of the *Tokyo Bar* logo (designed by Kashiwa Sato, who also designed the Uniqlo logo) resembles a regal red carpet. Inside, in contrast with the uneven, neon-licked syncopation of the manga frames, salvaged barn wood flooring and Edison ferment light generate warmth in the dimness between the 42-seat restaurant at the rear, and the more casual six-seat bar in front. In the rear, a powder-puff pink restroom riveted with rhinestones and other coy elements of the Otaku subculture was designed by Team Lab.

RUSTIC CHIC

02

Rustic chic is not just a response to global crisis or economic downturn, and it's not (necessarily) a political statement either. Finding the luxury in raw objects and rough environments is, rather, a turning away from the end-of-millennium bling, away from ostentatious luxury and the "convenience" of technology, and towards a contemplation of more simple things. This species of eating space is inspired by our trust for, and memory of, familiar objects. These interiors blend traditionalism with modernism, coziness with innovation, excess with austerity. They are marked by more neutral or subdued colors, and filled with objects that have stories or even a history; furnishings collected from a flea market or left by the previous owner, materials

 that can be picked up at any construction site, farm implements and old kitchen equipment, bare bulbs, naked unplaned wood. The colors of these interiors are the colors of the materials used to build them: grainy wood, warm brass, sheer sheets of plastic, foam scraps, and multicolored rip-ties. Surfaces are left unvarnished, unpainted, hardly finished, merely dusted with age, and then dusted off thoroughly to be put to a second (or

ninth) use. Back to the handwritten, back to carpentry! Go grab the glue gun! It is an era of uncomplicated shapes and less complicated lives. Bakeries and markets

have been swept up in the rush towards organic, local foods and the clarity and candor of their presentation. Restaurants whose interiors reflect this show respect for a time when we knew where our food came from and can provide escape from the idea of the city, if not from the city itself. It is inspired not by nature, but by living with nature. Sure, rustic chic may not bring diners and shoppers and coffee drinkers back to nature, but it may help bring us back to our senses. Behind "cabin culture" is the longing to rediscover a place in our heads that isn't hurried, overwhelmed, or terrorized; that isn't polluted or exhausted.

STUDIO ILSE
The Olde Bell Inn, 2007,
Berkshire / UK

Photography : **Lisa Cohen**

A stoically lush update of the traditional
English inn – you know the kind, which provides simple creature comforts, decent mattress-
es, an extra wool blanket, local chairs, local ales,
local cheese – by creative director and designer
Ilse Crawford. The Berkshire renovation will be
followed by other properties and was spurred by
Crawford's concept for the first modern coaching
inn. In the restaurant, she mixes traditional
Welsh blankets with Gebrüder Thonet, Ercol
and T-backed Matthew Hilton seating along with
the wholly contemporary Fold Lamp by Alexan-
der Taylor. Throne-backed booths are upholstered with blanket-like knits in subdued but
rich patterns and colors. Parts of the timber-
framed building date back to 1135, but the time-
worn quirks and creaky floors seem cozier than
ever, perfectly framed and enriched by the preci-
sion of Crawford's alterations and additions.

||[*] OPEN & SHUT → pp. 150

UXUS
Ella Dining Room & Bar,
2007, Sacramento / USA

Client : **The Selland Group** | Photography : **Mathijs Wessing**

In downtown Sacramento, California's be-leaguered state capital, this four million dollar, 710-square-meter interior has become "Sacramento's living room" (and bait in the city's plan to lure suburbanites back to the city). In former Gold Rush territory, with its strong ties to ranching and agriculture, the design was based around notions of "rustic luxury," which, defined by the architect, emphasizes the aesthetic purity, and beauty, of simple things. Ella's interiors indulge in the sensuality of real materials and real age, and try to recreate the comfort of dining at a dear (and filthy rich) friend's home. UXUS cast familiar objects in new roles, combining old with new, smooth with rough, inside with outside, and the humble with the opulent. A wooden tunnel-like entrance opens to a bold, bathtub-sized, hand-carved white Carrara marble oyster bar that cantilevers over a rough-hewn band of Belgian blue stone, wrapping the bar. Five hundred pairs of salvaged Hungarian farmhouse shutters form a canopy that frames the central bar, nearby walls,

and part of the ceiling, seemingly turning the restaurant inside-out. The lounge features generously tufted custom-made ottomans and reclaimed wood stools by Piet Hein Eek and ceramic Bufferlamps by Wieki Somers that fill the lounge with a low-slung arc of cables. In the main dining room, five-meter-high, linen-curtained columns punctuate and give scale to the voluminous space while hiding energy-efficient lighting. The design brings together indigenous hickory wood and solid elm with Kvadrat fabrics and wallpaper hand-screened with images of giant golden cutlery by English designer Tracy Kendall. The color scheme features neutral shades of bone white, natural linen, stone gray and taupe, with metallic gold and the patinas that only age can bring.

STUDIOS MÜLLER VAN TOL

Restaurant As,
2007, Amsterdam /
the Netherlands

Client : **Sander Overeinder, Koen Vollaers, Brian Boswijk** |
Photography : **Bart Nieuwenhuijs and Rene Mesman**

On the ground floor of a converted Amsterdam chapel and seminary, Studios Müller van Tol were inspired by rituals associated with eating and with religious relics when they conceived this tranquil, casual restaurant. With both indoor and outdoor seating, the spaces can be altered by staff or clientele when so desired. The space includes communal benches made from simple wood planks, rudimentary wall illustrations, and a completely open kitchen in a fenced-in area outdoors – an oddity for the rain-battered city. This was the studio's first project to forsake vivid color. The neutral shades defining the environment take their hue directly from the materials used.

ONNO DONKERS / OD-V

Bonanza Coffee Heroes, 2007, Berlin / Germany

Client : **Bonanza Coffee Heroes Berlin** | Photography : **Kiduk Reus**

Schiedam-based designer Onno Donkers collaged together existing objects to create a furniture series and, in the end, an interior for Berlin's *Bonanza Coffee Heroes* shop. The shop features seating, tables, and food display surfaces that Donkers assembled by perching MDF boards atop stacks of colored plastic crates. He bolted together his "pallet-bar" from a collection of wood scraps, pipes, and aluminum sheeting to provide surfaces of varying heights. The designer also culled together wall-mounted café tables from aluminum and existing desktops for an improvised aesthetic that gives the space a personality that is as strong as its coffee.

FRAUKE STEGMANN
Birds Boutique Café,
2005, Cape Town /
South Africa

Client : **Matilde and Heike Stegmann | Homage to Michael Marriott's exhibition at Camden Art Centre, London 2004**

Stegmann was asked to design a space that would reflect the humbleness and hard work that go into food growing and production; an interior that would allow the real food that *Birds Boutique* makes to speak for itself. "Real" food is what this café is about: food, supplied by small-scale organic farmers tending gardens and a few hens, and Moer coffee made camping style, that is only what it says it is. So the designer made certain that the interior reflects this in a raw way through its materials and exposed construction. "Although the gap between rich and poor in South Africa is now the largest in the world and the materials chosen for the interior all align with the poorer mass of the society, it wasn't to be gimmicky that I created a township look by

any means," Stegmann explains. "The utilitarian, low-key, do-it-yourself approach that in this country signifies poverty, is the ultimate clean lifestyle for the *Birds Boutique*." Stegmann worked with industrial materials produced locally and available in nearby hardware shops: plywood sheets, trestles, plastic crates, plastic cable ties, sheets of foam, unbleached linen, and wire mesh lockers. Up-ended crates become stools perched atop trestles, the plywood sheets became tables, foam was turned into cushions.

JASON FRENCH, BEN MEYER

Ned Ludd, 2008, Portland, Oregon / USA

Client: **Ned Ludd LLC** | Design/Build: **Jason French** |
Build/Design: **Ben Meyer** | Photography: **Cydney French** |
Iron Work: **Curtis Aric** | Plant Creations: **Artemisia** |
Craftsman: **Marcus Hoover** | Graphics: **M. Sean O'Connor**

Ned Ludd opened in a defunct wood-fired pizza parlor housed in an old barn. Design-build team Meyer and French focused their design on enhancing the existing brick-faced oven and transforming a hugely vaulted ceiling and large rectangular dining area into a convivial setting. They divided the space into three distinct dining areas with extra seats at the bar and built out the entrance using textiles and reclaimed wood beams to create a dramatic foyer. A drop ceiling over a portion of the dining room makes that section feel more intimate. Brass, wood, and recycled material became dominant throughout and finally determined the character of the project as "rustic/elegant." The designers took advantage of the city's Rebuilding Center and sourced metal locally from The Steel Yard, primarily from waste bins, hand forging or welding it to spec on site. Shelves were fashioned from kiln-dried pine, cut from a large tree that had blown down along a nearby inner-city highway. Bright colors, unique plants, rich fabrics, and culinary artifacts further softened and enlivened the space. They even used the original tables, chairs, and plates that they had inherited when they took over the space. The architects then called on a local network of Portland artists and craftspeople to finish out interior details, with the plan to change drapery and lighting details seasonally – all of which made *Ned Ludd's* interior echo the dynamic, creative forces at work in the kitchen.

48

TARA OXLEY
675 Bar, 2009,
New York / USA

Design: **B.R. Guest Restaurants** |
Photography: **Eric Laignel / www.ericlaignel.com**

675 Bar looks like the basement hideout of a young, unemployed bachelor with impeccable taste in design, enough pocket money to feed the habit, and a pitch-perfect articulation of 1980s nostalgia. Friends, who hopefully have just as much free time to kill as he does, go to his subterranean pad, with its vaulted brick arches and low-slung, library-filled niches, to watch movies, play Space Invaders or Miss Pac Man, shoot some pool, and drink a beer or two. Except instead of beer, 675 Guy serves, for example, the Algerian Typist (a folly of a lowball that involves tequila, Moroccan harissa, and a bouquet of pineapple, if you dare). His guests lounge on vintage furniture or drape themselves across the foozball table, engaged in a rather one-sided conversation with the Dutch Mr. Ed, a life-size horse-lamp manufactured by Moooi, who's stabled in a dark corner behind the billiard table. The surprising thing is this bachelor's appeal to all ages, genders and persuasions, but we must remember of course that he, and his space, were designed by a (very cool) girl.

PAOLA NAVONE
*Pane e Acqua Restaurant,
2006, Milan / Italy*

Client : **Pane e Acqua** | Photography : **Enrico Conti**

Paola Navone, who designed the adjacent Milanese design shop and cultural space owned by Rossana Orlandi, was invited to create a restaurant with the same spirit, mixing contemporary design and vintage pieces, industrial lamps and furniture. Navone worked to preserve the history of the building, which housed brick and tobacco factories starting from the 19th century. The walls were distressed to expose the different layers of finishes over time while the original floor was kept as-is. Navone mixed industrial vintage French furniture, old American tile coverings and 1950s British Shaker chairs and tables with contemporary pieces by Piet Hein Eek, the Eames's, and objects of her own design.

ABRAHAM CHEREM & JAVIER SERRANO

El Japonez, 2007,
Mexico City / Mexico

Client : **El Japonez** | Architecture : **Abraham Cherem & Javier Serrano** |
Landscape : **Guillermo Arredondo** | Furniture : **Jesus Irizar**

The textural poles of the *El Japonez* interior are a floor-to-ceiling installation of densely stacked blocks of wood and an adjacent living green wall. The play of shapes and tactility between these elements generates a strong identity for the space while its Eastern sensibility is suggestive of the food on offer. This visual personality was achieved through the development of a graphic identity that is suggestive of the organic, graceful, contemporary, and sophisticated forms that evoke Japan in the restaurant facade, menus, and advertising.

STUDIO
ARTHUR CASAS
Restaurant KAA, 2008,
São Paulo / Brasil

Photography : **Leonardo Finotti**

São Paulo is a city that reveals itself behind its walls. The discreet facade of the *KAA* gives no hint of what lies within: an escape from chaos, from the city into the jungle. Inside, the narrow space of 798-square-meters was given new depth through the addition of a hanging garden of plants from the Atlantic forest. The water mirror at the foot of the tropical green wall refers to igarapés, which are tributaries, streams that run from the Amazon. A huge stand at the bar divides the voluminous environment of the restaurant into two separate zones. And, of course, the canvas roof opens at the touch of a button at the first hint of palatable weather.

PETER WENDLING

Vercoquin — or How to Stay Sober, 2004, Lyon / France

Client : **SARL DTFS** | Furniture Design : **Jakob Timpe**

Sounding more like a morality play than a wine shop and bar, Vercoquin — or How to Stay Sober is located in Lyon's 7th arrondissement, where yuppies are blowing the dust off abandoned workshops and ateliers and transforming them into completely new spaces. Situated in a narrow, deep space that used to be a small delicatessen selling regional food and wine, the shop is a space in which things that are cheap don't look cheap. Except for some subtle colors, it was left as bare as possible, inhabited by only a few made-to-measure pieces of furniture. Peter Wendling developed a bookcase-like storage unit that he envisioned as the building block of a "wine library" and which covers an entire wall of the shop and can be seen from outside. The wine library, the bar, and a cash counter on wheels were made from pine plywood, selected for its rich veins, warm color, sturdiness, and low price; and because it paid homage to traditional wine crates that were also made from pinewood. A giant paper dome, made out of silk paper molded over a balloon using the paper-mâché technique, acts as a lampshade and accentuates the center of the shop. Otherwise, construction primarily involved glue and nail guns. Toward the rear, a floor-to-ceiling "felt scrub" separates the shop from the bar while acting as an acoustic absorber. Blackboards over the bar close the space visually towards the back and allow for clear display. At the other end of the bar, slender ribbons in three shades of green (imparted by an anti-moisture treatment typical of timber construction materials and protected with a simple wax finish) were arranged so as to reveal a tantalizing bit of the bar area, suggesting the obvious next step following the purchase of a good bottle...

BFS-DESIGN
Alpenstück, 2007,
Berlin / Germany

Photography : Annette Kisling

BFS rendered this cheerfully simple space in pale gray and white. The Mitte restaurant's assertively conventional looking tables and chairs are only background for a wall of chopped wood, stacked tightly together to form a warmly textural backdrop for a strong dose of comfort food. The look of the space was created in reference to the Southern German and Austrian menu, which lists traditional dishes from A to Zed. A is for Apfelstrudel. Z is for Zwiebelkuchen.

STYLT TRAMPOLI AB
Fjällpuben, 2008, Åre / Sweden

Client: **F12 Group** | Photography: **Erik Nissen Johansen**

Fjällpuben is the new establishment of star chefs Melker An-
dersson and Markus Aujalays, which was installed in Sweden's
most popular ski resort. Here, where exclusive restaurants sit
side-by-side with luxurious American-influenced ski lodges, the
two men decided to create a restaurant that could provide a more
authentic experience for guests; a modern but unpretentious, even
cozy "hangout" where big city ski bums would rub elbows with
local ski bums. Called simply "Fjällpuben" or Mountain Pub, its
interior and graphics emphasize simplicity and local tradition
mixed with playfulness and humor. Traditional cooking tools and
textiles were hung from the walls, local embroidery was incorpo-
rated, along with the colors of the provincial flag, the big blue sky,
the snow-covered mountains, and surrounding forests and mead-
ows. Needless to say, the walls, ceilings, and floors are lined with
plenty of rich, grainy stacks of cut wood and thick, dark planks.

URBAN RUSTIC
MARKET & CAFE
2007, New York / USA

Self-designed, Built by and Proprietors: **Aaron Woolf, Dan Cipriani, Luis Illades**

Finally, a market in the hipster-saturated north of Brooklyn that stocks the best of local farmers and producers, along with reliably made (read: a well-curated market!) staples from farther afield. *Urban Rustic* features biodynamic, organic, and sustainably produced food. The rough woods and crates, the handwritten chalkboard, say, "We know where our food comes from!" And you should too.

JOE CARROLL, ET AL

Fette Sau, 2007,
New York / USA

Client : **Joe Carroll & Kim Barbour** |
Photography : **Frank Oudeman 2009 © / www.frankoudeman.com**

Heaven for carnivores - *Fette Sau* means "fat pig" in German - this Brooklyn meat house serves "smoked meats, craft beer by the gallon, and has the best American whiskey list in New York City" (which makes it pretty competitive). Beyond a narrow storm fence and past a phalanx of picnic tables, a former garage opens up into tiled walls, a high ceiling, a floor that car mechanics would be familiar with, a row of tractor seats that serve as bar stools, and a set of 10 implements of the butchering trade (knives, meat mallets, and so forth) that act as draft beer tap handles. A long brick wall painted white has been illustrated handily with cuts of meat from cows, pigs, and lambs. The guy behind the counter wields an electric carver: ribs, pork belly, pulled lamb... As guests leave they would do well to wonder: who's the pig that's being fattened?

PHILIPPE STARCK
Mama Shelter,
2008, Paris / France

Client : **Mama Shelter** | Photography : **Francis Amiand**

In this Parisian hotel designed by Philippe Starck, in the rapidly gentrifying 20th arrondissement, each room is equipped with a kitchenette and, on *Mama Shelter's* main floor, refrigerators across from the reception make meals available to guests 24/7. The chef Yann Tanneau and Alain Senderens, responsible for the idea of such meals, also envisioned a corner with sweets to satisfy the sweet tooth of the youngest hotel residents. So food is pretty well covered here. The restaurant itself, with black chalkboard-like ceilings hung with copper saucepans and handwritten messages, pairs thick wooden tables and benches with a florid Louis XVI console table and is comfy-chic. This is Starck, slumming it gleefully.

KATI AND
MARCUS KÄSS

Käss Food & Pastries, 2008,
Düsseldorf / Germany

Client: **Kati Käss** | Photography: **Manfred Bartsch**

Downtown farming? The Kässes deftly
transferred the atmosphere of a rural farm into an
urban retail environment. They present high-
quality and healthy foods packaged and displayed
in natural materials as part of a rustic kitchen,
heart of the home concept. Despite its numerous
traditional elements, the store's various homoge-
nous gray tones and glazed wood stand in counterpoint to the rusticity and make an overall impression that is both graphic and modern. This is
a high-end snack shop concentrating on premium
biological produce that has captured the lunch
trade of local businesspeople because it offers an
attractive alternative to run-of-the-mill canteens
for the many creative workers in the fashion industry. This deli provides both take-out service
and space to eat-in, and has also become a place to
savor a quiet cup of coffee in the afternoon, once
the bustling lunch hour comes to a standstill.

SCALA WOHNEN, JAN SCHAWE
Mutterland, 2007,
Hamburg / Germany

Client: **Jan Schawe** | Photography: **Klaus Frahm**

The retro-modern Hamburg supermarket is all comforting rusticity: dark wood crates, old white tiles, and thick baskets. The homemade jam and house-brand coffee are popular, along with slow food ingredients, traditional German favorites, local potatoes, and wines. *Mutterland* reprises the postwar austerity aesthetic for those who are looking for authenticity and responsible living today. Local, healthy, handcrafted food becomes a design element in this space: the name of the bakery dusted onto its loaves in flour, handwritten tags on the condiment jars. This is a style and a mindset that avoids frills and gimmicks and instead seeks to strip away or pare down. Scrubbed wood mixes with pewter, recalling a time and a place when everyone knew from whence their food had come.

RICHARD HUTTEN STUDIO

Lloyd Bar in the Lloyd Hotel, 2008, Amsterdam / the Netherlands

Client: **Lloyd Hotel Amsterdam** |
Photography: **Daria Scagliola & Stijn Brakkee**

Designer Richard Hutten's bar in the public space of Amsterdam's Lloyd Hotel fits effortlessly into the architectural space created by architects MVRDV. In the primarily bright white hotel, Hutten combined both bar and shop, including food display, in a blackbox space where the bar, with its Lloyd Lamp, serves to illuminate the nearby restaurant, as well. This helicopter-like lamp sports criss-crossing "blades" that vary in height, length, and intensity. The floor-to-ceiling (and it's a high ceiling) wall cabinet, with a library ladder on tracks for fetching products from the highest shelves, functions as a shop that is a mix of hotel store and design shop. The food items, including preserves, chutneys, and muesli, are all "homemade" on the premises, using organic and seasonal ingredients. Since

many rooms at the Lloyd have no mini-bar, Hutten's big-bar is perhaps simultaneously necessary and delightfully excessive for the tourists, but the goods on offer and the atmosphere might even attract the locals.

KRISTIAN KUTSCHERA
Kafayas Café & Spécialités,
2008, Hamburg / Germany

Client: **Café Kafayas** | Photography: **Kristian Kutschera**

"I was asked to design a logo and ended up creating an entire interior," muses designer Kristian Kutschera of his adventure in creating *Kafayas*, part French boulangerie, part neighborhood deli, from flea market finds. Kutschera's new relationship to construction work came with the assignment to create a welcoming environment in a working class area that could offer the same high-quality coffee, sweets, and foods that were so easy to find in the trendier parts of town. By selling bread from a local organic baker, serving lunch, and offering a range of culinary products, it has become a lifesaver for locals all through the day. "Finding all the furniture and materials for the interior proved to be extremely interesting," the graffiti writer-turned-graphic designer admits, "and a creative learning experience in fields as diverse as carpentry and gourmet wholesale."

STRAIGHT-FORWARD

03

◆◇ Straightforward restaurant and food shop interiors celebrate the first purposes of the public food space: beyond providing flavor, selling comestibles in a lucid way that makes shopping easier, or showcasing a gem of a product, place, or Michelin-starred chef in a whitebox setting, as the aptly named Simplicity studio did with the gallery-like ORI HIGASHIYA sweets shop in Tokyo. All true, but these types of spaces provide more pervasive nutrients in our daily regimen: They offer a place to meet, the comfort of company, a way to break bread and break news to neighbors or even attractive strangers. Their lightly finished or even naked materials, the clear forms, the fewer (though still expressive) colors, the embrace of windows and terraces that look into greenery; all these give us a way to engage the senses beyond taste. Like comfort food, the reassurance they give lies in their candid simplicity. Sometimes unvarnished environments lend us new, unfamiliar space that isn't home, but where we can still feel at home, undistracted by doo-dads and uplighting and see-through rest rooms; as

Hemingway once wrote: "a clean, well-lighted place". These are boîtes that are just boxes, avoiding the pretention of five-star restaurants and the see-and-be-seen scenes that mar much of nightlife, making it so difficult to avoid gimmicks and cliché. They are based on one simple, strong idea. So much so, in fact, that one may not recall the look of the place once you have left it, but you will recall the feeling you had while in it, and it was a good one. Frank spaces appeal to those of us who do not necessarily want to escape or network or role-play to snare a mate; they are for those who want to savor good food and good company and share both. What you see is what you get.

AEKAE
Z am Park, 2009,
Zurich / Switzerland

Client : **Z am Park** | Carpentry : **Dylan Gregory** |
Photography : **Nico Schaerer** | Chairs : **Fabian Schwaerzler,
Fries&Zumbühl, Christophe Marchand / Christian Lehmann**

This location in a Zurich park offered views of trees and greenery; architecture studio Aekae didn't want to distract from this natural "design" element with a flashy, overwrought interior. Inspiration came from the classic Parisian park café, interpreted in an entirely modern way. In an effort to integrate the old and the new, the designers questioned the common perception and placement of materials, while being restrained in their use. Parts of the former floor, an oak herringbone parquet, were used to build the bar, couches, and wall benches, in a way that contrasts cheerfully with the warm, gray, monochromatic room. Materials were rescued and reused wherever possible; old curtains became upholstery, and a modular vintage lamp (by Trix and Robert Haussmann, 1965) was chosen to light the space. Aekae asked various artists and designers to re-work four of the classic Horgenglarus bistro chairs, which were used in the café for three months and auctioned off (profits going to the designers), making space for a new set of chairs – and a new twist to the interior – to follow.

E15
Xue Xue Institute,
2007, Taipei / Taiwan
Client · **Xue Xue Institute** | Photography · **Ingmar Kurth, Frankfurt**

The *Xue Xue Institute* is the first private academy in Taiwan that teaches students in the creative disciplines. The aim of the interior design by international design and architecture brand E15, with its fitted surfaces, built-in elements, lighting, and furniture, is to promote communication between the different groups that make use of the academy, moving away from lecturers standing at the front of an auditorium of note-scribbling students and towards lively exchange amongst peers, as a basis for creative learning and working. The entire complex of ten stories is structured like an open-plan loft apartment, in which people from different faculties come together and are able to design their own environments in a flexible and functional way, according to their requirements. This goal is already manifested in the institute's name, Xue Xue, meaning "learning, learning"; knowledge being passed from teacher to student and, not least, from student to teacher. With its ECOH kitchen lab, the *Xue Xue Institute* aims not only to bring cooking into the lives of its students, but also to engage and educate all the senses. Just as ECOH reflects an experimental yet original way of cooking and dining, the building's loft-like atmosphere and open kitchen-cum-living area and generous dining area are just as fresh and refreshing, as the guests and hosts who meet to prepare and taste food together.

PETER CORNOEDUS & PARTNERS
Carbon Taste, 2008, Genk / Belgium

Client : **Carbon Hotel** | Photography : **Hugo Thomassen**

Peter Cornoedus's choice of materials evokes the history of the local mining industry in the *Carbon* wine bar and restaurant. The architect relied on grays and blacks combined with a ceiling of mosaic tiles in warmer southern colors and illuminated the eatery with lighting created by Kreon and German designer Ingo Maurer. *Carbon Taste* serves contemporary regional dishes, prepared with regional and local produce, in the form of small bite-size portions. Each dish is prepared in an airy open kitchen in full view of the guests.

STANLEY SAITOWITZ, ALAN TSE

Toast Restaurant,
2009, Novato / USA

Client : **Brian Spiers** | Photography : **Rien van Rijthoven**

Toast, which serves comfort food for breakfast, lunch, and dinner, is located north of San Francisco, in a one-story Mediterranean kitsch mall encircled by an asphalt parking lot. Walking into the restaurant, one can see the toast theme immediately transferred to the interior design: the "yeast" that creates this dough-colored world is made from particleboard, perforated with amorphous holes, and covers most surfaces. The low, canopied entry turns into a 40-foot volumetric space with a hanging column suspended over the bar, containing storage for glassware. The bar below mirrors this cubic cu-pola, with seating on three sides. Behind the bar, the ceiling drops to the main dining area with large communal tables, smaller tables, and booths. The open kitchen has bar seating as well, and becomes an amphitheater for spectators watching the performances of chefs and pizza-makers. A fireplace with storage niches makes the interior feel, well, toasty.

WONDERWALL INC.

DEAN & DELUCA Seijo and Roppongi Stores, 2006 and 2007, Tokyo / Japan

Photography › **Kozo Takayama**

As local or regional retail ventures fan out across the globe, they must naturally decide which brand characteristics will travel with them. New York City's Dean & Deluca market and café has thrived in the northeast United States by reintroducing design elements that old-fashioned markets always had: the expertise, the imported and hard-to-find foodstuffs, the hand-picked produce, the artful pastries, and the refined housewares. In exporting this successful American concept to Japan, Dean & Deluca recruited Tokyo-based Wonderwall to help it fit in. The white-tiled and stainless steel Dean & Deluca stores still function as cafés but they've added a lounge in Seijo, with a large counter area that separates the two zones. The architecture firm preserved the old school glazed brick and stainless steel fixtures, modifying the spaces slightly to suit the Japanese market, adding buttery wood walls, for instance, and giving the shops an even greater lucidity and contemporaneity.

ASYLUM
Artisan Cellars Showroom,
2008, Singapore

Creative Director : **Chris Lee** | Design : **Ng Chee Yong** | Interior Design : **Cherin Tan** | Photography : **Edwin Tan (Lumina Photography)**

This wine cellar has become as much of a conversation piece as the wine it stores: 400 bottles of luxury wines. The bottles are contained in a 3 x 6-meter cement block that is extruded from the shop into adjacent public space. The design of Artisan Cellars, a high-end wine retail space specializing in small production vineyards, stands in contrast to other cookie-cutter cellars. Quotes from renowned writers – like Galileo Galilei's "Wine is sunlight, held together by water" – are etched into understated whitewashed walls while the simplicity and crispness of the surroundings give emphasis to the 10-seat tasting room, which will play host to a series of cozy wine tasting sessions. Asylum's cellar gives the wine the appropriate storage and a stage as well, but without distracting from the senses of those tasting it.

ARTHUR KOUTOULAS

Kafa Espresso Bar, 2006,
Sydney / Australia

Client : **Daniel Karaconji** | Photography : **Paul Gosney**

In the design district of Sydney, *Kafa* evokes the 1970s; with a futurist aesthetic fused with what designer Arthur Koutoulas calls "suburban kitsch nostalgia." Koutoulas approached the interior of the café like a stage set, using color, smell, sound, touch, and interesting props to make it atmospheric. *Kafa's* fluorescent green walls and large, round knotty pine table are crowned by a sculpted golden chandelier and ceiling. The light given off by the chandelier washes the "performers'" faces with a rich golden tone, making everyone look (and feel) warm and comfortable. "Our idea was really a small idea," says Koutoulas, "because we knew what we didn't want. We wanted it to feel like you had visited before, even if you hadn't, and to evoke a sense of past and future places." All surfaces were left raw, the architecture punctuated only with interesting objects: the bar, the chandelier, the exaggerated table (which seats up to 14 people). The custom-made furnishings are the stage props – and the stars – of the café.

CANTEEN

Canteen Baker Street,
2008, London / UK

Client : **Canteen** | Design : **Canteen In-house Design Team**

The design for *Canteen Baker Street* was done by an in-house team led by the restaurant chain's co-founder Patrick Clayton-Malone. With an emphasis on comfort and lack of pretension, Canteen's design philosophy was as much about quality and craftsmanship as its food philosophy. Clayton-Malone's inspiration came from the best historical examples that his team could find of communal, public spaces such as schools, libraries, town halls, and interiors that referred to the optimism of mid-20th century design, as well as the inclusiveness of community buildings such as the Royal Festival Hall. The interior, with simple colors and no-nonsense furnishings (that are now marketed as products under the label Very Good and Proper), celebrates honest materials – oak, marble, linoleum, cork, tweed – that ensure longevity and speak of both quality and democracy.

ARCHITECTS EAT
Maedaya Bar, 2008,
Melbourne / Australia

Client : **Toshi Maeda** | Builder : **Crown Shopfittings** |
Photography : **Derek Swalwell**

Maedaya demonstrates the possibility of using ordinary recyclable material for hospitality projects without compromising the sophistication of the design. Traditionally, sake is bottled in wooden casks and secured with ropes, a tradition which, like red or white wine, is now commonly being lost to the twist top. The designers created the two-story *Maedaya* by using simple natural materials (rope, timber, and concrete) and this traditional notion of 'binding" (which is typically applied only to shipping freight). On the first floor, the bar includes a space for a self-service grill and is seemingly bound with ropes in the shape of a house or hut. To accomplish this, the ropes were secured at one end, slung over a rod and held in tension at the other. Between the ropes, the team built timber sake lockers where patrons may stow unfinished alcohol for their next visit. The ground floor dining room stands in stark contrast to the rope-trussed bar and grill above: Here, the designers wanted to express an unembellished humbleness that would allow the function of the space to define it; with its whitewashed walls, black-stained timber flooring, simple timber benches, and raw stainless steel canopies, it is clearly a space for enjoying good food and good company.

CURIOSITY
Ana Crowne Plaza Hotel,
2008, Osaka / Japan

Client: **Ana Crowne Plaza Hotel** | Design: **Gwenael Nicolas /
CURIOSITY** | Photography: **Nacasa & Partners**

The "graige" (gray and beige) tone of this Osaka hotel café combines natural stones and washed wood, highlighted with metallic sculptural lighting behind a ceiling. This combination of backlighting, diffuse light surfaces and pinpoints with these materials imbues the space with a sense of modernity, tranquility, and luxury. The contrast between the different zones – exposed and intimate areas – also creates a second "menu" of space from which diners may choose. In the center, presented on large stones, a generous buffet provides the focus of the space and perhaps the focus of a little meditation with the meal.

SIMPLICITY
ori HIGASHIYA Sweet Shop,
2005, Tokyo / Japan

Client: **ori HIGASHIYA** | Design: **SIMPLICITY / Shinichiro Ogata**

The *ori HIGASHIYA* gift shop is dedicated to *wagashi,* the traditional art of Japanese sweets and confections, and is located, quite appropriately, on the ground floor of a gallery complex showcasing contemporary Japanese design. Focusing on the Japanese tradition of gift giving, the shop proposes not only the gifts themselves, but their presentation as well. At the front of the shop, traditional wooden gift boxes and paper folding techniques are displayed to give decorative texture to the walls and to welcome guests. This area functions as a shop where sweets and housewares may be purchased. Behind the shop is a salon where plaster walls and rice-papered ceilings recall an austere, though comfortable, traditional tea room in which patrons may enjoy tea, sweets, and various alcoholic beverages, including liqueurs infused with local fruit and herbs.

[A] — Facade
[B | D] — SABO (tea room)
[C] — Shop

[A]

[C]

[B]

[D]

TAKAHIRO FUJII
Konjaku-an, 2009,
Osaka / Japan

Client : **Konjaku-Kobo Co.,Ltd** | Design : **inly products** |
Photography : **Seiryo Studio**

This bakery, old-fashioned preserved foods store, and coffee shop produces fresh handmade bread daily, using domestic wheat and a concoction of different organic ingredients every day, and serves a traditional Japanese lunch. Architect Takahiro Fujii sought to bring contemporary and old school Japanese culture together in this interior while keeping it very new. To evoke the "old days," Fujii salvaged vintage items: an old running board, a worn-out farm implement, an antique table, a bamboo colander, and so forth. To update this collection of objects, he mixed them with modern elements: the dome of an umbrella, construction site lighting, a hula-hoop that he turned into a wall partition. It was important to Fujii that this interior was not the product of new technology. Instead, it features existing, banal objects in new uses and contexts, giving visitors a fresh perspective on what is familiar.

STUDIOS MÜLLER VAN TOL

Tampopo, 2006, Amsterdam / the Netherlands

Client : **Wiebe Mokken** | Graphic Concept : **Dirk Laucke · Studio Laucke** | Photography : **Gregor Ramaekers**

Unlike the typical Asian food stores (or tokos) in Amsterdam, where it is often difficult to find the right product, *Tampopo* has a clarity that translates to good cheer. Amsterdam is full of small Asian stores and tokos. They are cheap and charming, but often chaotic. Shoppers need to know exactly what they are looking for and it often takes a visit to more than one store to complete the shopping list. In the meantime, conventional supermarkets offer a limited number of Indonesian, Chinese, and Japanese products. This gap – between the rich but chaotic assortments and the limited, shallow collection of merchandise – is exactly where *Tampopo* is positioned. Besides having a vast inventory, *Tampopo* offers ready-to-eat snacks that can be eaten at the counter or taken out. Bas van Tol's interior concept features white glazed tiles with rounded edges throughout the space, including the surface of shelves and counters. Despite the profusion of choice, the white porcelain makes shoppers feel as if it wouldn't be improper to eat off any surface in this immaculate little market.

Stay or
Take away

Sushi
Soep
Loempia
Bapao
Viskoekjes
Lemper
Dadar Gulung
Pekingeend
...

ONTHETABLE
Gemma Cucina,
2006, Rome / Italy

At first glance, the forms of this restaurant make it appear to be a typical old Italian trattoria, but a simple design concept transforms it. In a word? Stratification. Walls, tables, chairs, and almost everything else is colored in bands, as if the interior had been dipped into three huge vats of color. Even the menu and the change tray follow this rule. From the sidewalk to the first 10 centimeters inside the door, the color is turtledove; after 120 centimeters, it graduates from turtledove to white. The main character of the space is red. This was born out of the owner's decision to have a scarlet Berkel antique meat slicer in the restaurant. Therefore, lamps too have been given red wires, along with armchairs in the hall and second dining room which have been upholstered in red. Like the Berkel slicker, vintage was honored as part of the concept too: many items are vintage, including the placemats and old framed images.

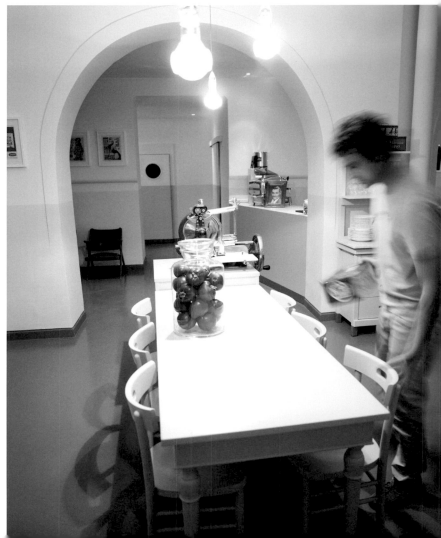

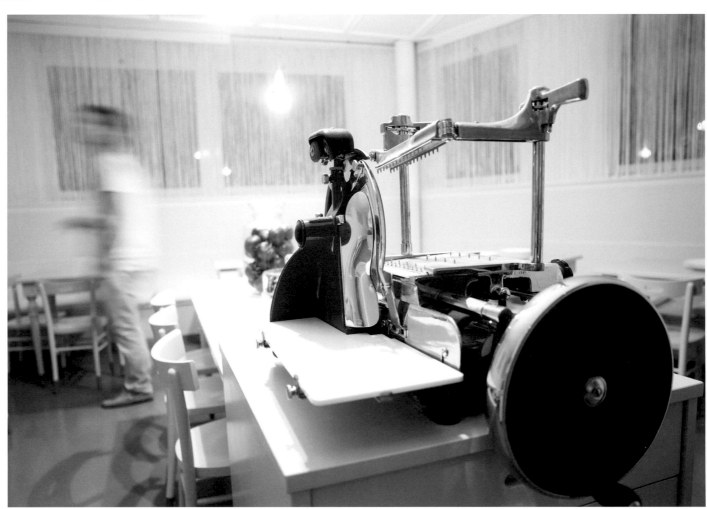

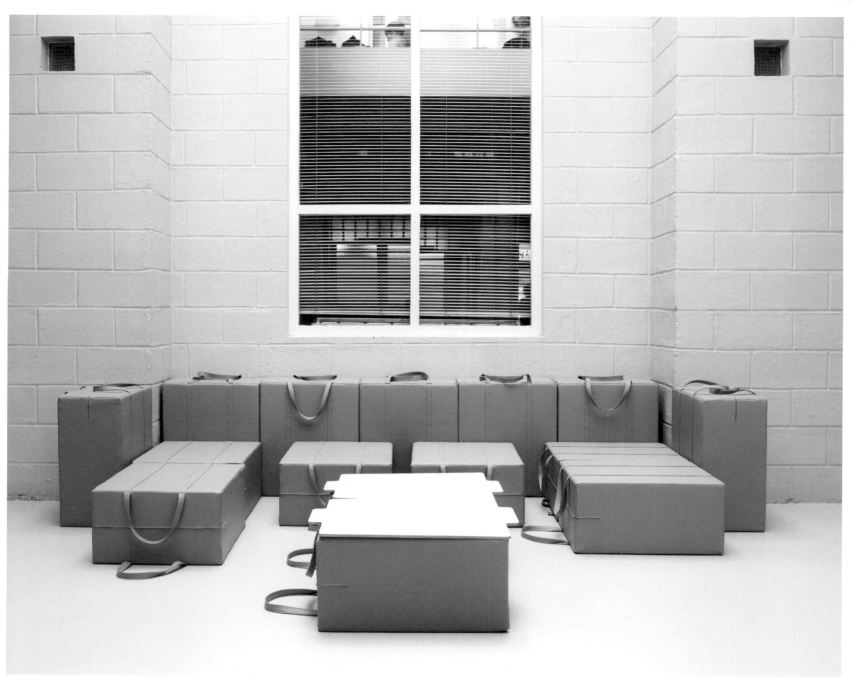

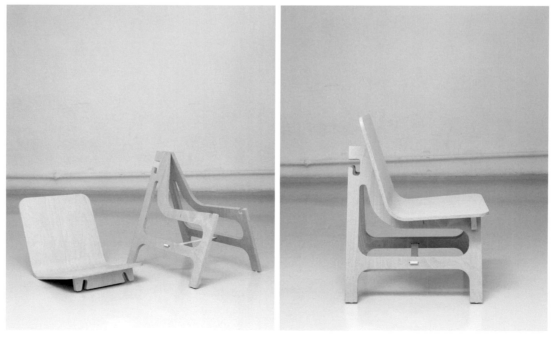

MATALI CRASSET

La Cantine de la Ménagerie de Verre (The Glass Menagerie), 2008, Paris / France

Photography : © Jérôme Spriet, Patrick Gries | Instant Seat, Instant Table : **Moustache** | Hi-pouff : **Domodinamica**

The Glass Menagerie, "an experimental factory" devoted to multiple art and design disciplines, has added a cafeteria designed by Matali Crasset. "I tried to retain its breathing, its evanescence, the reasons why one likes it," says Crasset. "It is an ethereal space where time has no hold and this is why my intervention is discreet." The reception room that Crasset was asked to redesign serves as a place to relax, to wait, to take refreshment before or after a show, when a company is working and is in residence. The place demanded serenity and so Crasset chose smooth, unassertive birch plywood. Around a cellular wooden structure, islands of tables, low armchairs and pouffes are arranged, offering two types of comfort. The armchair and the table take their cues from the trestle and are pieces that have been produced for the label Moustache. This device allows furnishings to be removed at any time to free up the space for various projects. The unusually low table is conducive, Crasset explains, to conviviality.

93

MUT-ARCHITECTURE

Restaurant 51, cinémathèque française, 2009,
Paris / France

Client: **Hughes Piketty** | Scenography: **Le Potager Design** |
Photography: **Brigitte Bouillot** | Construction: **Kunstbetrieb**

Restaurant 51 sits within the Cinémathèque Francaise, which is housed in a Frank Gehry structure completed in 1994. Pouring from the building, a forty-meter-long picnic table meanders outside and then wanders back in again. The wooden structure is bent and shaped to seat the greatest number of people, with half the table extending outdoors and facing Parc Bercy, and the other half arcing through the interior of the restaurant. The table enters and exits the building in a virtually seamless line, cultivating a sense of sociable communal dining, inviting people from the park and adjoining neighborhood.

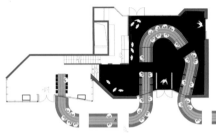

[A]

[B]

[A] — Restaurant 51 sits within the Cinémathèque Francaise, which is housed in a Frank Gehry structure completed in 1994 at 51 rue de Bercy, in Paris's 12th arrondissement.
[B] — Inside the restaurant, the épicerie is an amalgamation of discarded furniture pieces purchased for 250 euros. Working on site, MUT and Le Potager dismantled the furniture, cut away shelves, smashed through drawers, chopped off certain legs, then crunched the remaining parts together to fit into the space allotted for it.
[C] — The second turn of the table sweeps through the main dining room, creating a communal space.

[C]

RO&AD
ARCHITECTEN
Sober, 2008, Amersfoort / the Netherlands

Client: **Peter & Caroline** | Photography: **Anita Huisman**

RO&AD created a concept for a restaurant in a former Opel showroom. The clients support traditional craft, and wanted to work with like-minded suppliers, which is ultimately reflected throughout the space. Putting on display the naked beauty of a bare-bones structure, the space includes: made-to-measure bars and a kitchen; silver-plated hospital cutlery that pairs well with the china; and a unique furniture line consisting of chairs, stools, tables, and lamps CNC-milled from sheets of plain birch plywood. The legs and arms of the chairs are stabilized by screwing on a four millimeter seat and back. The lamps are made from folded 0.4 mm birch multiply, cut so thin that the light shines through and, in the evening, the adhesive in the multiply gives the shades a lovely red glow.

FRANCESCO MONCADA
Pizza Perez, 2008,
Syracuse / Italy

Client : **Vincenzo Perez** | Design : **Francesco Moncada** |
Graphics : **Point Supreme** | Photography : **Alberto Moncada** /
www.albertomoncada.com

Usually the construction is forgotten when a building is finished, but at this pizzeria on the ground floor of a 1970s-era building in the business district of Syracuse, construction materials are naked and beautiful. A teensy budget freed Francesco Moncada to use materials most typically seen on a construction site. The resourceful architect clad the ceiling, a partition, and the storage wall with a type of fiberglass usually used in garage doors, and the kitchen floor and wall in shipyard plywood, while the bar is an assemblage of metallic painted boxes that provide an anchor for steel shelving. Cubby holes in the transparent fiberglass wall are used as an informal display for wine, ingredients, and tools used by the restaurant, and as a wardrobe for diners' coats and bags. On top of this, the speaker and air conditioning systems are hidden.

The design emphasizes the social aspect of eating out. Usually, tables and chairs allow guests to sit in inward-facing groups, while interaction between groups is not facilitated. To combat this, Moncada minimized the volume occupied by a single table (a 70-cubic-centimeter cube) and the distance between tables. The dining room is illuminated by circular and linear standard neon, which is typically used in garages.

The colorful Damien Hirst-like wall graphics by Point Supreme are as simple as the space: All the ingredients used in the pizzas on the menu are mapped and indicated by colors and codes. Combinations of colors and codes result in the various pizzas. This precise and scientific-looking matrix covers the wall in the seating area. The pizzas are exhibited and arranged according to season, providing an abstract overview of all the menu possibilities.

Also painted on the wall adjacent to the entrance, a life-size zebra provides a visual, colorless counterpoint to the scientific information, while refusing to offer any explanation of its presence. "It is simply standing there beautiful, mysterious, surreal," Moncada says, "inspiring endless discussions amongst the customers waiting for a table or take-out food."

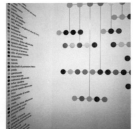

AC ARQUITECTOS
Clínica do Pão (Bread Clinic),
2005, Lisbon / Portugal

Client : **Private** | Architecture : **Joao Tiago Aguiar** |
Photography : **Joao Tiago Aguiar - acarquitectos**

Its designers treated Lisbon's *Bread Clinic* like a medical intake where visitors can heal hunger. This allowed them to organize functional areas along this theme: waiting room, operating table, sterilization area, or kitchen and prep zone (a stainless steel box), and the rubbish and contaminated products zone or the W.C. (a red cylindrical volume to its infectious nature). They signaled the function of each zone via simple hospital colors – white, black, red – bisected with a long pocket ceiling light that runs nearly the length of the space and recalls a light that might be in an operating theater or emergency room. Although AC used a metaphor for the interior that is usually far removed from the serving of a sandwich, they abstracted it so successfully that they made it genuinely useful to the functionality of the space without making it visually (or gustatorily) distracting.

EFGH
*Dogmatic Gourmet
Sausage System,* 2008,
New York / USA

Client : **Blum Enterprises** | Steel Fabrication : **Chris Otterbine** |
Photography : **Kelly Shimoda**

The design of the 600-square-foot interior
and storefront for the new flagship lunchbox
Dogmatic is based on the aesthetics of butchery.
A 14 x 4-foot communal butcher-block table
serves as the focal point of the space, and incorporates clever retractable cantilevered seating to
avoid any freestanding furniture in the tiny
space. A raised, built-in banquet on the west
wall provides the base for the Sausage Wall of
Fame, while a mural describing the *Dogmatic*
story is baked onto its ceramic tiles using a trans-
fer toner technique. The 11-foot-tall vertical glass
menu screens a portion of the open kitchen,
while hanging off a steel armature from the restaurant hood. Light cylinders on tracks are suspended from meat hooks and a pair of steel
storefront doors pivots to allow for maximum
openness and connection to the curb.

IPPOLITO FLEITZ GROUP

WGV Cafeteria, 2008,
Stuttgart / Germany

Client : **Württembergischen Gemeinde-Versicherung a.G** |
Photography : **Zooey Braun**

The company dining hall didn't just come about because there were no alternatives or because employers were trying to keep employees in the building (and working) over the lunch hour. Neither do they always turn a profit for the company. But if the "cafeteria" were to become a pleasant "café" with decent food and a visually stimulating environment, it could inspire fruitful lunch conversations and give worker bees a bigger buzz for the rest of the day. The design of the staff cafeteria at the WGV insurance group headquarters by local architects Ippolito Fleitz achieves just this. The cafeteria is split into two areas: a dining room proper and a self-service area, where a propeller-shaped standing table with three protruding tabletop surfaces lit by three minimalist, halo-shaped lights creates a dynamic first impression of the cafeteria. A large black chain curtain partially obscures an unattractive view behind it while defining the space. (The vending machines that typically dominate this type of environment with their heterogeneous display windows are hidden behind stainless steel panels.) In the dining room, various seating scenarios accommodate different types of social or work meetings: a suspended standing counter in the corridor at the entrance; a "restaurant car" with eight compartments containing elevated booths that run the length of the facade; and the centerpiece of the cafeteria, seven round tables that are laid out on overlapping circular areas. Over each table, a dome-shaped suspended ceiling is illuminated indirectly using reflecting panels. A bronze-colored partition made of curving wood lamellae makes another set of tables feel more intimate.

EXTRASTUDIO
Delicatessen Fugas Lusas,
2007, Setúbal / Portugal

Client: **Rogério Silveira** | Project Team: **João Ferrão, João Costa Ribeiro, Madalena Atouguia and Sónia Oliveira** | Contractor: **Sérgio Cachão unipessoal lda** | Photography: **João Morgado**

Extra was commissioned to create a Portuguese delicacies shop that would also work as a café. Combining these two complementary functions required the creation of a unique space that could be as extraordinary as the products the client was proposing to sell, and as cozy as a neighborhood café. They opened a large shop window, exposing the café to the square, in anticipation of a future terrace. New shelves were carved on the thick exterior walls to display a wide range of products. The bar, clad with typical Portuguese ceramic tiles, divides the working areas from the public space. What distinguishes the project are the laser cut plywood ceiling panels, the pattern of which is duplicated on the counter's tiled sides. A set of used hardwood chairs was preserved from the old assembly room of Setúbal's Fish Industry Union, to go with marble-topped tables from Alentejo.

Café in Sintra, 2008, Sintra / Portugal

Client: **Seara da Serra II, Lda.** | Project Team: **João Ferrão, João Costa Ribeiro, Andreia Teixeira, Filipa Ferreira,Maria João Oliveira, Tiago Pinhal Costa, Maria Amaral Hidraulic** | Consultants: **PRPC Engenheiros** | Acoustics: **Acustiprojecto, lda** | HVAC: **Frivenco, lda** | Contractor: **Costa e Costa, lda.** | Photography: **Extrastudio, João Morgado**

In a residential suburb outside of Lisbon, this café took its inspiration from the nearby Sala de Musica (Music Room) in the Palácio de Queluz and from the early 20th century patisseries and cafés, where the elements that most strongly characterize the interiors are completely independent from the structure in which they have been inserted. This means that the formal and tactile universe created here would be as distant as possible from the nature of the existing building, a generic suburban housing block. Tadelakt lime plaster, polished stuccos, colored cement tiles, mirror, and ruivina, a local marble: these were the ordinary materials used. Generated through a morphing sequence of computer models, however, the main space was the result of the union of several different sections: the existing rear-windows, a new vaulted space, and the entrance. Brought together, these created a seamless, continuous transition between walls and ceiling. Structural elements, entrances, refrigerated showcases, and all fixed equipment were embedded in the thick walls, introducing a "character" with a strong personality into a neighborhood with very little character.

PERFORM

04

Today, eating out is more deeply experiential than in compliance with the gestures and dictates of mere etiquette. Eating designer Marije Vogelzang, for example, questions etiquette, itself: by choreographing eating experiences, she throws a measure of serendipity into her recipes and perhaps, in the end, gives her guests the relief of catharsis. Restaurants have long used the tropes of theater to cultivate baroque social rituals around food. Nowadays, dining out is as universal a form of recreation and escape as theater ever has been. Scenography and staging, graphical and architecturally acrobatic spectacle, and sometimes an almost vaudevillian confusion of performer and audience generate a sense of play around food

 that restores something forbidden to us from our early childhood. One mustn't play with one's food after all. Or should we? Today, designers use a palette worthy of Aristotle's "Poetics" to bring the palate – and eating space – to life: plot, character, themes, and reversals. What drama! Who expects to eat dinner at a table suspended from the sky (well, okay, a very tall crane)? This species of interior (and exterior) is sometimes

ephemeral, lasting anywhere from a night to a year; convertible, opening and closing like a flower at the push of a button; or mobile. Eat in a former train carriage or a salvaged shipping container. Or dine in a tree house. These interiors spark performances in our heads, inspiring flights of fancy; or place us on a stage of the surreal, even offering, like Bompas & Parr, an alternate

means of consumption. Inside their misty ALCOHOLIC ARCHITECTURE, visitors drink Hendricks & tonics through their eyeballs, not their gullets. Other eateries bring a fiction to life: Marti Guixé's FOOD FACILITY makes a virtual concept (the search engine) physical by creating a restaurant where all the food on the menu is ordered from and made by other restaurants. They ask, as every good playwright should: what is possible?

[A]

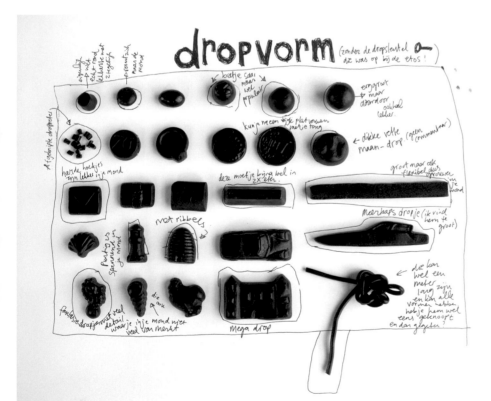

[B]

[C]

[D]

MARIJE VOGELZANG
Proef, Amsterdam /
the Netherlands

According to Marije Vogelzang, food is already perfectly designed by nature; the world doesn't need any more "food designers." Vogelzang works with both design and food, but she calls herself an "eating-designer" instead, choreographing a product that is predicated on the verb "to eat." Unique perhaps in the world of product design, Vogelzang's materials of choice are all things edible. She works with chefs as master craftsmen, just as another product designer might work with a plastics technician to develop a new chair. By cooking up lollipop pistols, tablecloths made of bread dough, or soft sweets for toothless seniors, she asks her guests to chew on the origins of food, its preparation, etiquette, history, culture – and our relationship with it. Vogelzang is the creative mind behind Netherlands-based Proef, a food laboratory and eatery whose name means both "to taste" and "to

test" in Dutch. Proef serves seasonal, organic, and local foods for breakfast, lunch, and high tea, for which the staff keeps hens (Arianne, Anastasia, and Elena) and grows much of its own produce. Vogelzang also choreographs eating experiences that require that guests explore topics ranging from health and memory to etiquette and war. "There is no material that comes as close to human beings as food does," Vogelzang points out. It is often thought that designers who work with food only design the shape of the food. Vogelzang's aim is to look at the content, background, and beliefs that surround eating. The shape of our meals is just a tool to tell the story. "You put my designs inside your body," she says.

[E]

[E] — On arriving at Proef Rotterdam for the Elements dinner, guests were served food based on their astrological sign.
[F] — At the launch of Vogelzang's book EAT LOVE, questions were written on every egg shell like, Would you actually taste it if food is made with love? When was the last time someone fed you?
[G] — At a launch party for London's Bare Magazine foods that make those eating it smell and taste good were presented on a wall of spoons.
[H] — Watercress as a salad topping.

[F]

[I] — Proef served "forgotten" vegetables at Droog Design's Open Borders exhibition in Lille.
[J] — For Vogelzang, a dish is a composition and tastes are musical notes that compose a 'musical piece' in the mouth.
At this event, guests ate small bites of food in a particular order and in time to the beat of a drum.
[K] — Proef, the "eating design" studio in Amsterdam.

[G]

[H]

[I]

[J]

[K]

DUS
ARCHITECTEN
City Mug Dinner, 2008,
Amsterdam / the Netherlands

Client : **Iittala Group – Helsinki** | Photography : **Eisa Sjelvgren, DUS**

DUS Architects' temporary food performance served to launch their two "Amsterdam City Mugs" in collaboration with Iittala. The studio's two limited-edition mugs were inspired by Kaj Franck's 1952 Teema design and based on the city's coat of arms, as well as the windows of the houses along its famous canals. "You can get a great introduction to the city's story by looking through the windows of its houses," says Hedwig Heinsman of DUS. "Amsterdam residents are well-known for not pulling their curtains in the evening, and they often place their most treasured items on display in their windows." This fading local tradition, and the dialogue between the street and private domestic space which it

represents, inspired a number of "secret" events held in different locations around Amsterdam. Each event took place close to (or even on the sills of) the city's windows, which tested how easily public spaces and people's private spaces could be brought closer together. The last stage of the project took place at the Iittala flagship store in Amsterdam. For one night, DUS designed a food performance inside the shop, transforming its interior by creating an 8-meter-long cooking island that provided food and drinks for 150 Amsterdam residents. Soup, ice cream, and bread were prepared in the mugs and in front of guests and served directly to them.

KEUKEN-CONFESSIES / FRANKE ELSHOUT & MAARTEN LOCKEFEER
Food Cabinet, 2009,
Eindhoven / the Netherlands

Photography : **Romy Kuhne, Josef Blersch**

Inspired by the way that animals and insects are stored and displayed in natural history museums, Elshout and "creative cook" Maarten Lockefeer built a curiosity cabinet of comestibles. The goal was to demonstrate the natural beauty of food and the objects used to contain and serve it. An almost office-like cupboard showcased a different dish or a different method of organizing small appetizers in every drawer. Ceramics were arranged like shells tied together with cotton rope and baked. A series of glass bottles morphed from a cocoon shape into the body of an insect, the liquid inside creating a different impression in each.

LUCY + JORGE ORTA
70 x 7 The Meal, act VIII
Aspen, 2001, Colorado / USA

An installation for 448 guests in the form of an outdoor communal meal.

70 x 7 The Meal, act XXVII
Medical Foundation for the
Care of Victims of Torture,
Albion, 2007, London / UK

The artists created an installation and charity dinner for 99 guests at the Albion Gallery London, including special place-settings and centerpieces. The proceeds were donated to the Foundation.

70 x 7 The Meal, act L City of London, 2006, London / UK

Photography: **Anna Kubelik** | © 2010 by Lucy+Jorge Orta

The Ortas designed an open-air dinner for 8000 guests in the City of London. The table runner measured several miles and started at the Tate Modern, spanned the Millennium Bridge beyond St. Paul's Cathedral, then ran along King and Queen Street through the city to the Guildhall London.

BOUROULLEC BROTHERS
Textile Pavilion : the restaurant,
2006, Luxembourg / Belgium
Design: **Paul Tahon and R & E Bouroullec**

The new Museum of Modern Art Luxembourg (MUDAM) opened in 2006 in an I.M. Pei-designed building with a museum shop and restaurant perched under one of its tall glass roofs. The Bouroullec brothers, who made these two spaces in the exquisitely spare manner that is typical of them, sought to counteract the strong direct and reflected light entering the space and create a congenial atmosphere within a monumental stone interior by offering islands of shelter. Early in their career, the Bouroullecs had already begun to build micro-architecture, a mixture of furniture and shelter that offered a perfect solution for this project. The result was a pair of stand-alone, human-scale pavilions, breaching the vertical geometry of the interior in order to create an atmosphere of domestic comfort. Paired with the epic architecture, the pavilions serve as soft refuges because they are clad with the brothers' Kvadrat modular textile tiles, which are hung like pelts over two robust wooden skeletons. The restaurant pavilion contains two long tables made of Douglas fir, which seem to levitate between rows of Thonet chairs. Its clear tinted tile ceiling seems to be the meeting point between a blue morning sky and the beige Bourgogne stone floor, while its shadow protects diners from the sun. Like padding, the thick tiles absorb sound to create a muffled, intimate atmosphere, like a children's fort writ large. Similar to a Mongol yurt, the tiles can be assembled via a folding system that requires no external mechanical fixtures or adhesives. Four lateral slats are inserted into the slots of adjacent tiles, lending rhythm and volume to the resulting wall. It is an architecture that looks as organic as a lizard's scales.

JERSZY SEYMOUR
First Supper / Mak Vienna,
2008, Vienna / Austria

Design : **Jerszy Seymour Design Workshop** | Photography : **Peter Kainz**

During Vienna Design Week, Seymour's First Supper workshop at the Museum for Applied Arts & Contemporary Art (MAK) invited museum visitors and design "amateurs" to create the environment in which they would dine. Instead of focusing on the creation of a final product (and commodity), Seymour allowed non-professionals to celebrate the act of making an interior from wood, multicolor, melted resins, and other materials. Guests designed and then dined: around plywood trestles, resin tabletops, and benches; in their own fleeting social, culinary, and design utopia.

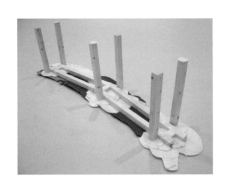

viva La utopia

REMIKS
Supermarket Store, 2008,
Belgrade / Serbia

Client : **Slavko Markovic, Kovac Group** | Design : **reMiks (Maja Vidakovic Lalic, Marko Basarovski, Mihajlo Juric)**

The concept for this Slovenian supermarket promotes slow shopping and healthy eating enriched with various experiences. The flexible space can be easily reconfigured to suit various cultural events and encourages the inventive showcasing of food and other products to beneficially influence consumers' decisions. The store is designed to generate greater and more effective interaction amongst shoppers, displays, clerks, and information about brands and responsible living. Most engaging, a luxurious kitchen laboratory makes the cooking process visible to guests, tempting them with fresh innovative multiethnic dishes that change throughout the day; from breakfast, brunch, lunch and snacks, through dinner.

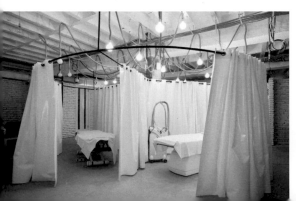

ECAL
Cucina Festiva, 2003, Milan,
London, Barcelona, Lausanne

Teacher: **Ronan Bouroullec, Industrial Partner: Boffi S.p.A.** |
Design: **ECAL / Adrien Rovero, Sibylle Stœckli, Edouard
Larmaraud, Raphaële Zenger, Pierre Fantys** |
Photography: **©ECAL/Anoush Abrar**

As its reference point, this project takes a
scene with which we are all more or less familiar:
the large festive gathering – somewhere between
the family reunion and director Marco Ferreri's
1973 film La Grande Bouffe, about suicide by hedonism. The project consists of a generic rent-a-
kitchen, comprising an interior that can be rapidly constructed and serves simultaneously as
kitchen, table, bench, working surface, and market gardening display. In this cheerful scenario,
the focus comes to rest on the preparation of both
food and festivity: production is thus the heart of
the party. The design of all these elements and
their easily inferred uses make *Cucina Festiva*
strikingly theatrical while taking the ubiquitous
concept of the communal table one step beyond.

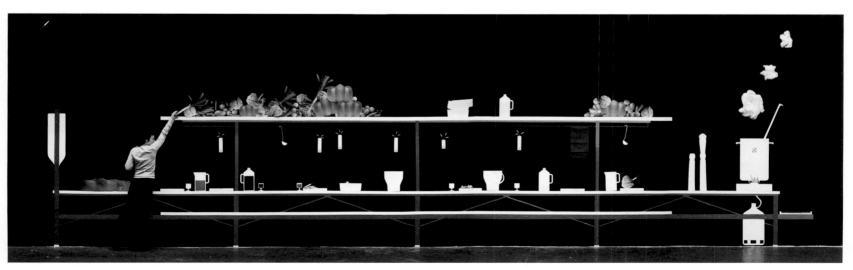

PAOLA NAVONE
Richard Ginori@Taste Lounge,
2009, Milan / Italy

Client : **Richard Ginori 1735 and Pitti Immagine** |
Photography : **FuoriSalone**

Navone's design of the temporary *Taste Lounge* reinvented Italy's oldest porcelain manufacturer in the form of a rest stop, café, and coffee house for Milan's Salon del Mobile fair attendees. The *Taste Lounge* featured "Il mio piatto preferito" (my favorite dish), a café whose menu was created by food design collective Arabeschi di Latte. The lounge featured an international collection of design-fashion-lifestyle magazines which guests were invited to browse whilst catching their breath on the cushy sofas. Navone imagined the voluminous industrial interior as a stage for the Ginori 1735 collections, including porcelain from the factory, color test plates, dishware whole and stacked in rows on industrial planks that were used in the kilns – as if cooling from the oven, or broken to make tiles for a mosaic. It also featured porcelain created by Navone as part of the Bon Souvenir project, a limited edition of commemorative plates based on historical dishware that was once dedicated to memorializing special events, places, and anniversaries.

MARTÍ GUIXÉ

Candy Restaurant, 2007, Tokyo / Japan

Presented by: **Yurakucho Marui and Marunouchi – Café Ease, Tokyo 2007** | Concept / Art Director: **Marti Guixé** | Creative Director: **Morihiro Harano** | Executive Producer: **Osamu Enari** | Food Cordinatior: **Kyoko Hirosawa** | Copywriter: **Hidetoshi Kuranari** | Design: **Yusuke Kitani** | Producer: **Ryuji Ueno, Koji Fujioka** | Account Executive: **Hiroyoshi Sako** | Agency: **Drill Inc. / Dentsu Inc.** | Production: **Hoseisha Co.,Ltd / Partners Inc.** | Client: **Yurakucho Marui** | Photography: **Imagekontainer/Knölke**

Candy Restaurant is, as the name suggests, a place for eating candy. The space is configured like an ordinary restaurant, with a preparation area where the candy chef organizes the dishes and a dining room with a round table and seats for eating sweets in a formal setting. The candies are served on a white dish in a highly graphical fashion that has been Guixé's signature for a number of years. The configuration and writing on the plate serves as a menu (with a choice of four menus), as well as instructions on how the gem-like meal should be eaten. According to Guixé's concept, *Candy Restaurant* formalizes the occasional act of eating sweets by creating a ritual for it that mimics that of everyday, any-time-of-day consumption.

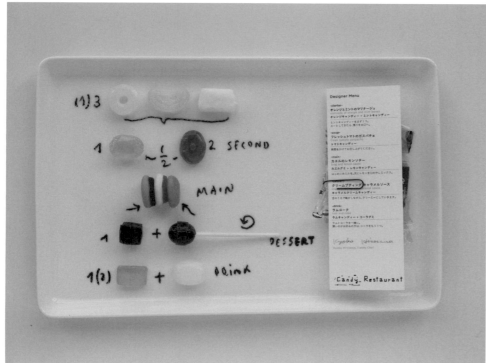

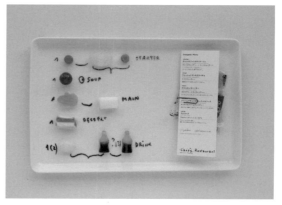

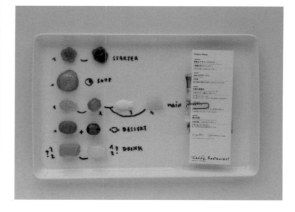

120

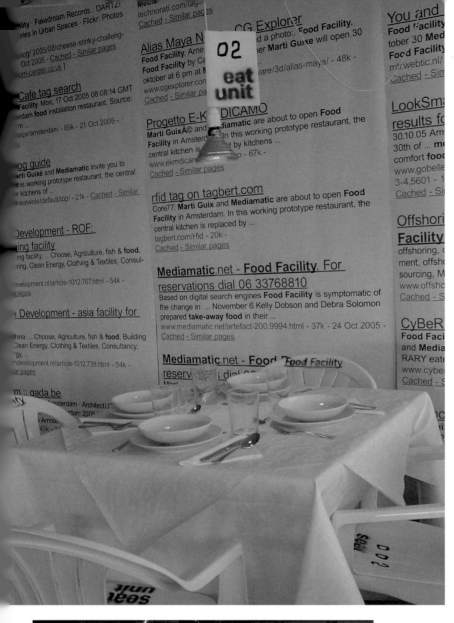

Food Facility, 2005, Amsterdam / the Netherlands

Client : Mediamatic | **Photography :** ©Imagekontainer/Knölke

Food Facility is a prototype restaurant that made use of a kitchen outsourcing system in order to offer its customers "more than nine kitchens and lots of drinks," says designer Martí Guixé who splits his time between offices in Barcelona, where he was born, and Berlin. For Guixé, whose entire career has seemed devoted to finding new approaches to design and contemporary (over)consumption, *Food Facility* was also a prototype for a new business model. Commissioned by Mediamatic, Guixé brought the virtual potential suggested by search engines like Google or Yahoo into the physical world. With a blue linoleum floor and walls papered with Google search results for the terms "Guixe" and "Food Facility," the aptly named eatery re-placed the typical central kitchen with the kitchens of existing take-out restaurants nearby. Guests chose from the menus of those kitchens and then the take-out was delivered to, and consumed on, the premises of *Food Facility*. The concept included: a Food Host; a Food Adviser, who like a waiter counseled diners on the quality and average delivery time of various local take-out restaurants and then placed the order on their behalf; and a Food DJ, who received the delivery, removed all packaging materials, and gave the order to the Food Adviser, who then delivered it to the table. As Mediamatic suggested, there was room for serendipity to occur at *Food Facility*, just as there is during a Google search: if diners were willing to do a little wheeling-and-dealing with guests on either side of them (or even across the room), it was possible to enjoy a bowl of Tom Ka Ka as an appetizer, spareribs as an entrée, and tiramisu for dessert. It's a brave new world, if one isn't paralyzed by all the options.

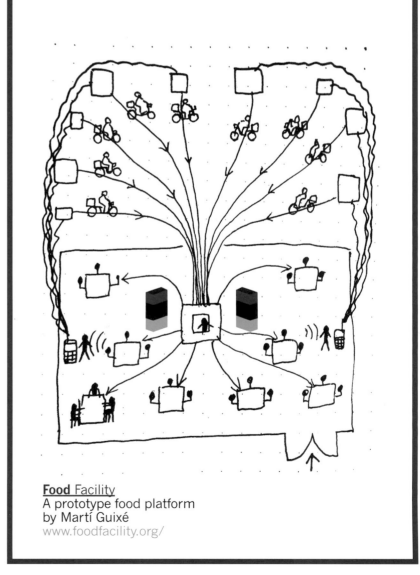

Food Facility
A prototype food platform
by Martí Guixé
www.foodfacility.org/

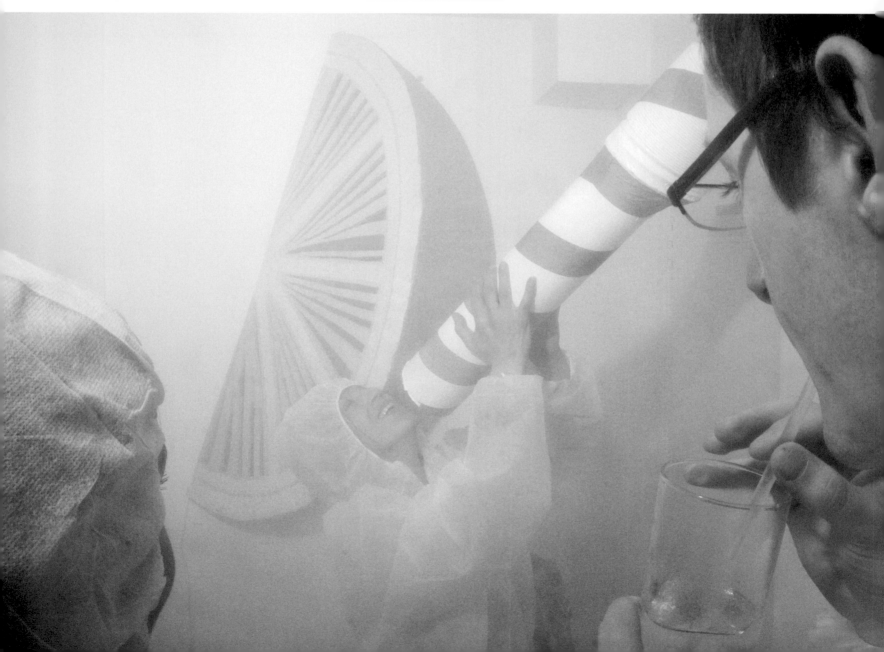

BOMPAS & PARR
Alcoholic Architecture, 2009,
London / UK

Photography: **Dan Price, Greta Ilieva**

A bar made from breathable booze? Bompas & Parr created a temporary installation enveloped in a cocktail cloud that was cinematically surreal. The pair's work usually operates in the space between food and architecture, exploring how taste may be altered through synaesthesia, performance, and setting. For *Alcoholic Architecture*, they concocted their vaporous lowball from a recipe of Hendrick's Gin and tonic water that was then diffused throughout. The interior was designed to suggest to guests that they were actually inside a cocktail garnished with gargantuan limes, massive straws and a soundscape created by artist Douglas Murphy. After one hour inside Alcoholic Architecture, experts estimated that visitors would have imbibed the equivalent to a large gin and tonic with the spirits entering the bloodstream through the lungs and eyeballs, instead of the mouth. "We had to work with three different doctors," the designers explained, "to make sure the H & S was tight on this."

[A] Chopping block — CHINA, Hong Kong
[B] Grill — UGANDA, Kampala
[C] Coffee wagon — ARGENTINA, Buenos Aires
[D] Market stand — CHINA, Hong Kong

124

MIKE MEIRÉ
Global Street Food,
2009, Cologne and Weil
on the Rhine / Germany

Client: **Dornbracht Edges Exhibition series** |
Photography: **Hartmut Nägele, © Dornbracht**

[F]

Meiré's 200-square-meter *Global Street Food* exhibition was dedicated to the curator's fascination with improvised kitchens in public spaces across the globe. Urban fast food stations must function in the smallest of places and either close up, or move away easily. Meiré presented a variety of objects and street foods in beautifully bare vignettes, underscoring their sculptural and cultural qualities. Taking food environments out of context – some of these objects appeared almost to have been silhouetted in a 3D version of Photoshop – allows viewers to look at the elements from which they are improvised from different points of view: Instead of being blind to another street food kiosk, they may ask, What materials is this made from? Where do they come from and how do they work together? At its best, this method allows us to rediscover elegant and timelessly clever solutions that have been lost in our long march toward sophistication and convenience.

[E] Lollipop stand — ARGENTINA, Buenos Aires.
[F] Cheese and sausage stand — ARGENTINA, Buenos Aires
[G] Floating market — VIETNAM, Ho Chi Minh City

[E]

[G]

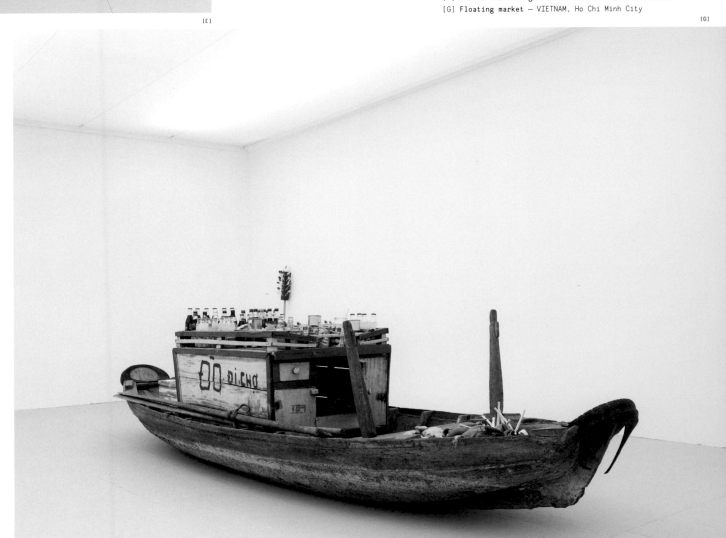

KEUKEN-CONFESSIES / FRANKE ELSHOUT & MAARTEN LOCKEFEER

Sustainability, 2007, Eindhoven / the Netherlands

Client : **Philips Design** | Design : **Franke Elshout/Keukenconfessies & Snodevormgevers** | Photography : **Josef Biersch**

The brief from Philips was to create a supper around the idea of sustainability. Franke Elshout and "creative cook" Maarten Lockefeer design "total food experiences" – from location, furniture, and interior to the preparation and presentation of food – that revolve largely around the social aspects of eating. The designers approached every part of the meal from a different notion of sustainability. Instead of soda, they served tap water with fruit syrups, and no meat. Elshout grew vegetables in pots and harvested only what was needed, with the plant returned to the garden proper following the meal. "I enjoy placing food in a different social context," Elshout says. "More than the cooking techniques, it is interesting to play with the expectations that people have in regard to food. Often I am guided by contrast, industrial versus craft, business versus casual – worlds very far apart are able to connect through food."

MARTIJN ENGELBREGT

Rest., 2008, Wageningen / the Netherlands

Client : **Beelden op de Berg** | Photography : **Hans Dijkstra**

Rest. was a temporary open-air restaurant that served food made only with leftovers and edible vegetation. Martijn Engelbregt built *Rest.* by stacking 45 picnic tables vertically to form a vast pyramid. The name of this picnicking structure is short for Restaurant but also refers to the Dutch word for "leftover" and the English meaning of "rest," as in relaxation. On Saturday afternoons, the staff visited market stalls, garden allotments, local bakeries, and other small shops to collect ingredients. Because most of these ingredients would still be good to eat on Sunday when most shops were closed, and would have gone bad by Monday, the items collected would otherwise have been thrown away. On Sunday mornings, local experts took guests on an "adventure trail" hike to identify and harvest any edible wild plants in and around the park in

which *Rest.* was located. All the food collected (both weeds and leftovers) was then used by food artist Miguel Brugman to prepare innovative meals like bread lasagna and blackberry-muesli puree dotted with edible wildflowers. The meals, which people could eat inside the picnic-table pyramid, were served in a bento box (a Japanese lunchbox). On days when the café was closed, the staff provided an alternative: a vending machine filled with the ultimate slow food, raw potatoes, ready to be planted.

ASIF KHAN
West Beach Cafe, 2008,
Littlehampton / UK
Client : **Jane Wood & Sophie Murray** | Photography : **Hélène Binet**

West Beach figures as Khan's first commission, immediately upon graduating from the Architectural Association in 2007. The award-winning project is part of the architectural rejuvenation of the south coast of England alongside the distinctive East Beach Café, designed by Thomas Heatherwick. The brief was to create a fish and chip restaurant on a miniscule budget and a 7 x 7-meter site at the meeting point of the English Channel and the River Arun. The result is a compact, multifunctional building inspired by a child's dollhouse. It is designed to make a virtue of the unpredictable English weather by allowing staff and customers to easily alter its convertible structure, varying its degree of openness and panoramic views throughout the year. A row of six oversize Victorian sash windows on the facade swing open, giving the building subtle changes to its appearance and its ventilation. Its 1200 kilogram facade is hinged like a doll's house so that it can be swung completely open, drawing in the sea air and creating a protected exterior space for dining or events. Customers may eat in the restaurant or on the beach outside and the raised interior can also double as a stage for concerts, turning the shore into a blue-vaulted auditorium.

LETTICE DRAKE AND PALOMA GORMLEY
Frank's Café, 2009,
London / UK

Client: **Hannah Barry Gallery** | Engineers: **Price & Myers** |
Furniture Design: **Guy Gormley and Chris Raymond**

Frank's Café was commissioned by the Hannah Barry Gallery to accompany the summer sculpture show Bold Tendencies III. Situated on the roof of a 10-story car park, the café took in panoramic views of London from the Millennium Dome past Big Ben and from the London Eye to Crystal Palace and served light lunches, dinner, and cocktails through the end of the summer. The structure consisted of nine 50-meter long ratchet straps that looped around the entire floor plate, lashing a bright red PVC canopy to the car park roof. Each strap was supported by a trio of timber columns constructed from reclaimed scaffolding planks bolted together. The café used a minimal material palette; the structure, bar, and furniture were all made from the same reclaimed timber. Interestingly, both structure and furniture were constructed over the period of one month by volunteers with little or no experience. Meanwhile, the roof and ratchet straps were fabricated in a factory that produces drop-down canvases for commercial trucks. The project was a collaborative venture; conceived, constructed, and run by a group of friends.

RAUMLABOR-BERLIN & PLASTIQUE FANTASTIQUE

The Kitchen Monument,
2006 – 2008, Europe

Design: **raumlaborberlin / Jan Liesegang, Matthias Rick & Marco Canevacci /Plastique Fantastique** | Photography: **raumlaborberlin & Marco Canevacci, Rainer Schlautmann**

The Kitchen Monument is a mobile artwork and social stage. The zinc sheet-clad sculpture houses a membrane that can be extended into public space. This pneumatic spatial mantle transforms it into a temporary, sheer, balloon-like pavilion in which various programs may be staged at different locations. Its broad spectrum of uses includes a banquet hall, conference room, cinema, concert hall, ballroom, dormitory, boxing arena and, most beautiful of all, a steam bath. Views out through the membrane are slightly blurred and distended, giving the thin layer of shelter a feeling of robust strength and resilience against wind and warrior alike.

STEPHAN KERKHOFS
Dinner in the Sky, 2006,
Mobile concept,
28 countries and growing

Client: **Varies by event: Nokia, S.Pellegrino, American Express, Renault, etc.**

This mobile communal dining table can be suspended at a height of 50 meters from a crane to host breakfast in the sky above Istanbul, lunch in the sky above Budapest, cocktails in the sky above Cape Town, or a corporate meeting or Internet coffee klatsch over London. Designed to conform to rigorous German safety standards, the table accommodates a staff of up to five people at its center and can be booked for up to eight hours anywhere (golf course, castle estate, vineyard) with a ground surface area of 500 meters. Caterers in the sky have served everything from lobster and sushi to tapas, or hosted wine tastings. Guests must be 150 cm or taller to attend (wearing 4-point seatbelts with a turning capacity of 180 degrees) and they will find infrared heating, but no toilet facilities, in the air. Instead, when a diner inquires of his waiter where he might find the restroom, the entire table, guests included, is lowered in less than a minute. Another well-considered aspect of the design? For those litigious Americans, *Dinner in the Sky* has secured an extra 10 million US dollars in liability insurance.

PACIFIC ENVIRONMENT

Yellow Treehouse, 2008,
Auckland / New Zealand

Client : **Yellow** | Architect : **Peter Eising** | Project Managers : **The Building Intelligence Group – Gareth Skirrow, Blair Wolfgram, Joe Holden** | Engineers : **Holmes Consulting – Chris MacKenzie & John Worth, Martin Feeney – Holmes Fire** | Building Contractors : **NZ Strong – Shane Brealey, Paddy Molloy, Megan Roberts; Citywide Construction Ltd - Jim Bellamy** | Timber Fins : **McIntosh Timber Laminates – Owen Griffiths, Sandy Sandiford** | Lighting : **ECC Lighting & Furniture – Renee Kelly** | Equipment hire : **Hirequip** | Crane : **NZ Access - John Morrow** | Earthmoving : **C&L Sorenson - Carl Sorenson** | Timber : **Timberworld** | Hardware : **Master Trade** | Restaurant fit out : **Carlton Party Hire** | Catering : **Dawsons - Graham Dawson Roofing PSP** | Photography : **Lucy Gauntlett**

Yellow Pages commissioned Pacific Environments Architects to create an unconventional and temporary, but fully functional, restaurant in a 40-meter-tall, two-meter-wide redwood tree. On a site that rises above an open meadow and meandering stream on the edge of a wood near Auckland, this temporary tree house recalled childhood dreams, playtime, and fairytales while being unabashedly grown-up. Its shape was borrowed from multiple forms found in nature: the chrysalis, a seashell, or a garlic clove hung to dry. Pacific also envisioned it as a lantern, a glowing beacon at night that, during the day, is partly camouflaged by the canopy of surrounding trees; and as a tree fort that offers both vista and refuge. Guests access the restaurant via a 60-meter walkway in the treetops – an adventure in itself.

The site and tree were selected in order to host 18 seated guests and wait staff with a complete bar, with kitchen and toilets situated at ground level. (Oddly, since it had to be filmed to create adverts for the client, Yellow Pages, there also had to be space for cameramen to create good shots.) The café itself forms a simple oval wrapped organically around the trunk and anchored structurally at top and bottom. Timber trusses provide the main structure with weather-resistant acrylic sheeting on the roof, glue-laminated, curved pine fins, plantation poplar slats and redwood (milled from the site) walkway balustrades. Voids left between the slats/fins became the windows and, to interrupt the regularity of these elements, steel ribbon was wrapped around the pod. Visitors had the sensation of being cocooned in the space, but the envelope was actually porous, offering treetop vistas and, on a "Juliet" deck opposite the entrance, a view down the valley.

ART HOME
Nomiya / Palais de Tokyo,
2009, Paris / France

Client : **Electrolux / Palais de Tokyo** | Design : **Laurent and Pascal Grasso** | Photography : **Kleinfenn**

This temporary, movable restaurant on the roof of Le Palais de Tokyo Museum in Paris takes its name from a diminutive restaurant in Japan. A glass cabin with a perforated metal screen covering the central cooking area features a dining room for twelve people and a panoramic view over the Seine and Eiffel Tower. The 18-meter-long structure was partially constructed in the Cherbourg boatyard in northern France and transported to Paris in two parts, where it was assembled on the roof of Le Palais de Tokyo. Colored LED lighting was then placed between the metal skin and glass core, staining white Corian furniture with light in the dining room. The culinary concept, designed by chef Gilles Stassard, offers diners a new menu each day for a full year. No surprise then that, with the advent of temporary projects like *Nomiya* (and, previously, the traveling Hotel Everland), the roof of the Palais de Tokyo has become a much more popular destination.

DANIEL NOISEUX
Resto Muvbox Homard Des Iles,
2009, Montreal / Canada

Photography : **Pascal Lavarenne**

Talk about a movable feast: Daniel Noiseux recycled a marine shipping container to build an efficient, mobile restaurant that functions almost off the grid. Noiseux, trained in architecture and graphic design, brought the first wood oven pizza to Montreal, Canada in 1981 as Pizzaiolle. The *Muvbox* concept offers gourmet fast food that moves, well, fast: each day the box can be opened or closed in 90 seconds at the touch of a button, like a cubic robot awakening or being put to sleep. Since it is not anchored permanently to the ground, Noiseux needed no building permits and installed the restaurant in its inaugural location, on the promenade waterfront area in Montreal's Old Port, an area frequented by tourists and business people. He can move it anywhere by road, rail, or sea with relative ease, and without being bound to a large truck cabin that must be stored nearby, taking up space. Resto, which serves simple dishes, local Brome Lake duck, and lobster from the nearby Îles-de-la-Madeleine was envisioned by the designer as a modern reinvention of the old school canteen. Except that it is green, too: powered by solar energy, it generates 40% of the energy it consumes, utensils are made from biodegradable plastic and packaging from recycled paper, and diners walk on floors lined with salvaged tire rubber.

ADAM KALKIN
Illy Café, 2007, Mobile

Client: **Illy Coffee** | Engineer: **Quik Build** |
Photography: **Luca Campigotto**

This mobile café for the Illy coffee company blossoms like a flower by simply pushing a button. Kalkin conceived *Illy Café* as a variation of his previous Pushbutton House 1, a five-room home complete with kitchen, dining room, bedroom, living room, and library, all of which he folded cleverly into an ISO freight container. This closed container unfolds hydraulically into a public coffee bar. The core of the container becomes the café where guests may sit at a long table with a small library of books and a chandelier. The bar, with no less than three espresso machines, inhabits an end of the container, which also conceals all the wiring for the bar. To the left, workspace includes a desk and computer, as well as a washroom. To the right, the lounge consists of a sofa and side tables. The predominantly white interior was accessorized with a white awning to shelter the exterior flanks of the container during inclement weather but, when the bar is closed, a tiny Illy sign serves as the only evidence that this shipping container is something other than it seems.

STUDIO MYERSCOUGH

The Deptford Project,
2008, London / UK

Client : **Cathedral Group** | Design : **Morag Myerscough / Studio Myerscough** | Handpainted Train by : **Morag Myerscough** | Furniture Design : **Morag Myerscough and Luke Morgan** | Elvis Toilet by : **Luke Morgan**

"Make happy those who are near and those who are far will come," reads the exterior of the train carriage that is *The Deptford Project*. Hand-painted by British designer Morag Myerscough, the train has been dusted off and dressed up to serve as a raucously graphical eatery. Inside, Myerscough printed plain white stools with black text in various typefaces on sitting-related subjects: Save My Seat, I Saved This for You, and Rear of the Year, among other things. They hem the edges of a long communal dining table finished in different colors and textures and illuminated overhead by brilliantly fringed pendant lamps. Underfoot, particleboard flooring is set off by paper-white walls and ceiling. All of the furniture was designed and fabricated by Myerscough with Luke Morgan, who also designed the establishment's Elvis toilet.

LEYLA SAFAI
Heartschallenger, 2006,
New York, Los Angeles,
Miami / USA

Heartschallenger is a 21st century "lifestyle brand" that uses small pink ice cream trucks to spread the word about the do-it-yourself spirit that it promotes. The blushing trucks ply the streets of Los Angeles, Miami, and New York stocked with treats from around the globe, including (but not limited to) international sweets, ice cream, jewelry, limited-edition clothing, mix tapes, vintage dead stock sunglasses, glitter guns, and so forth. The *Heartschallenger* concept was born in the Mojave Desert during a pre-dawn rave party in the early 1990s. The owner envisioned an innocent little ice cream truck pulling up in the middle of nowhere and providing all the kids who yearned for something more in their lives with magical treats.

JIMENA GONZALEZ, JEROME CHANG

DessertTruck LLC, 2007,
The Streets of
New York City / USA

Client: **DessertTruck LLC** | Design: **Jimena Gonzalez, Jerome Chang** | Photography: **Jenica Miller**

New York City's first gourmet mobile food truck roams the streets striving "to make thoughtfully-made food affordable and accessible." Brought to life by a trio that includes Le Cirque's pastry sous chef, the award-winning mobile patisserie sports a logo and truck-wrap graphics by Jimena Gonzalez. Though truck-based food service is nothing new to New Yorkers, bringing office workers and school children alike anything from coffee and ice cream to dumplings and jewelry (a high-carb "meal" to some Manhattanites) *DessertTruck* has refreshed the concept by serving high quality food off its chassis.

[A] — slow-baked apples with puff pastry, cranberries, crumble, and whipped cream
[B] — bomboloni with vanilla cream filling
[C] — warm chocolate bread pudding with bacon creme anglaise, whipped cream, and chocolate tuile
[D] — vanilla creme brulee
[E] — goat cheese cake with rosemary caramel, fresh blackberries, and vanilla tuile
[F] — molten chocolate cake with olive oil ganache, roasted pistachios, and sea salt
[F] — coffee mousse, mascarpone cream center, chocolate sauce, cocoa puffs

[A]
[B]
[C]

[D]
[E]
[F]
[G]

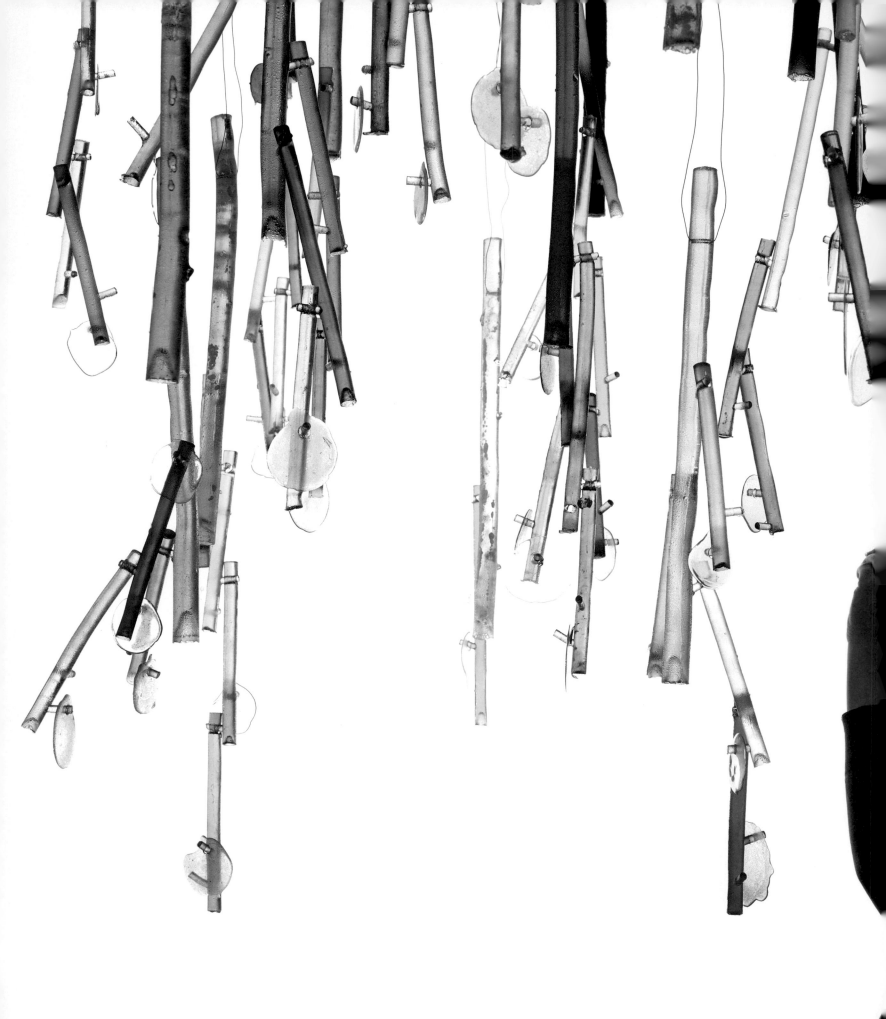

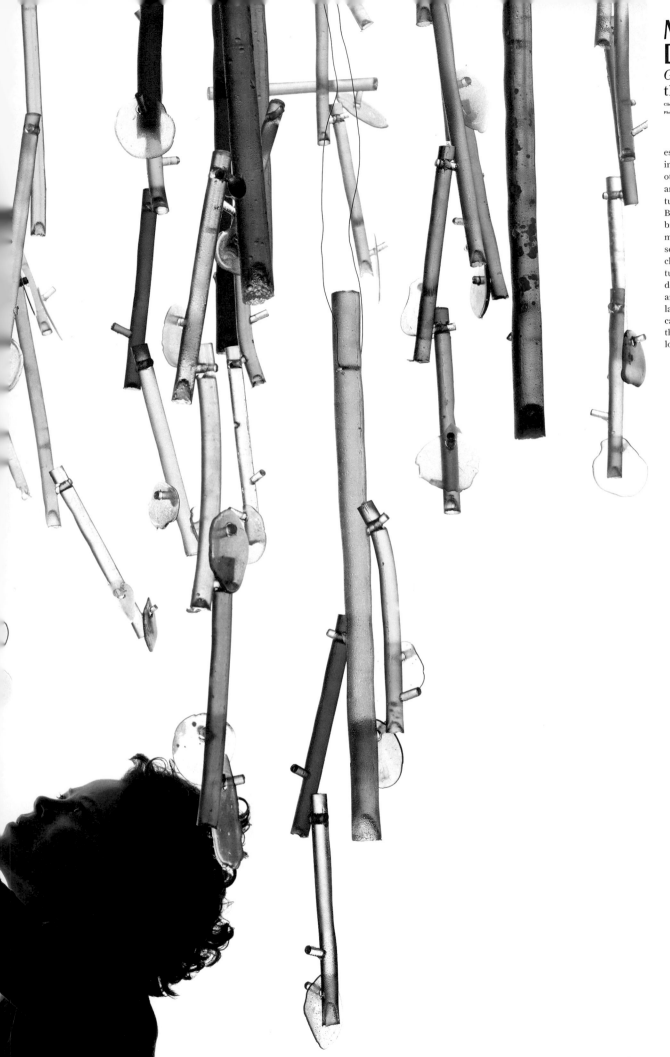

MARIEKE VAN DER BRUGGEN

Garden of Delight, 2008,
the Netherlands

Client : **Graduation Project Design Academy Eindhoven |**
Photography : **Rene van der Huls**

In the *Garden of Delight*, a candy-hued forest descends, sparkling like icicles from the ceiling. The branches resemble popsicles, fruits, and other sweets, tempting visitors to pluck them and taste. "I have been fascinated by the structure and production of sweets," says van der Bruggen, who cast the tinted abstractions of branches in silicone moulds, using sugar to make the entire garden edible. "It's amazing to see how sugar, during the production process, changes gradually both in hardness and structure and has the same appearance as glass." Van der Bruggen experimented with numerous sugars, colors and flavors in her studio, settling at last on a recipe that produced a tasty, resilient candy that was still delicately aesthetic. Forget the kids. Which adult doesn't regularly long to lose themselves in the woods?

OPEN & SHUT

05

Some restaurant interiors are designed to foster personal experiences and interaction. This can involve proximity: guests at the chef's table actually sit inside the kitchen to enjoy a real exchange with the people who are preparing their meals. Or it can be about taking one's dinner in a private dining room that is separated to some degree (by walls, porous partitions,

screens, or sliding glass doors) from the main restaurant. Designers may simply open the kitchen to views from the restaurant floor, allowing clients to at last see, if not take part in, the action. Marcio Kogan's FORNERIA SAN PAULO gives the eyes clues to where the action is: the sheerness of soft curtains and a large glass wall that forms a TV screen over the kitchen invite the gaze even more readily because they are paired with (beautiful but opaque) visual dead ends: wood panels and a tiled floor. In the white-tiled BOTTEGA LOUIE, a vast glazed downtown space is dotted with chefs and bakers mixing up a batch of macaroons, brewing the coffee, and arranging mozzarella on a slab of dough before nudging it into the wood-fired

oven. In other spaces, these more private chambers formalize the separation of the group from other diners in the restaurant, putting the focus on the social experience as much as the food. These quiet, contained spaces are usually more restrained in the intensity of their lighting (although the chandeliers are never very "restrained"), more conventional in their elegance, and slightly subdued in color. It is a restraint perhaps that allows diners to leave theirs at home.

BLACKSHEEP
High Table, 2008,
London / UK

Client: **Neil Walkington** | Photography: **Gareth Gardner**

Blacksheep transformed the ground floor of The Eastgate Hotel in Oxford into a new 90-cover restaurant with private dining area and bar. The destination spaces were designed to be flexible and suitable for day-to-night use in order to generate maximum revenue, as well as to attract non-residential customers. In the front, the long black bar dotted with black pendant lamps with gold interiors and a naked wood-plank floor feels both rich and pragmatic. The private dining room features gold feather printed wallpaper on a black ground, half a wall devoted to wine display and storage, a comfy tufted silk sofa, and a heavy, gilt-framed mirror – condensing the establishment's refined gentlemanly comfort into something more sensuous.

PROJECT
ORANGE
Whitechapel Dining Rooms,
2009, London / UK

Client : **Whitechapel Art Gallery** | Photography : **Richard Bryant**

The influential Whitechapel Art Gallery gave UK debuts to the likes of Picasso, Rothko, and Pollock. Project Orange created the new dining rooms as part of the gallery's ambitious expansion plans, doubling the size of the gallery by extending into the historic Victorian library next door. The approach synthesized the history and character of the original Arts and Crafts building, and the contemporary cutting-edge character of the exhibited works. In contrast to the expansive gallery spaces, these public areas are intimate and cozy, characterized by their timber paneling, pendant lighting, and leather upholstery. Reclaimed library units contrast with modern detailing, fixtures, and fittings. The result is a space that seems at once modern and traditional, and where the materials will change and improve with age and use. Perhaps the most important use for the private dining room designed by Project Orange? Its role as the place where bread is broken: to build trust and deepen the relationship between gallery owner and art collector (and, when needed, possibly between artist and gallery owner). The rules of hospitality dictate that guest and host are bound to each other by certain rules of etiquette. The art world certainly needs some rules, if not the etiquette.

uxus
Ella Dining Room & Bar,
2007, Sacramento / USA

Client: **The Selland Group** | Photography: **Mathijs Wessing**

In a restaurant that has become "Sacramento's living room," in former Gold Rush and ranching territory, *Ella* was designed to evoke "rustic luxury." *Ella's* interiors rely on the sensuality of real materials and sometimes salvaged materials contrasted with the most modern of elements; wedding the humble with the opulent. The private dining room is sheathed in wallpaper, hand-screened with images of giant golden cutlery by English designer Tracy Kendall, draped with soft linen curtains, and brought together around the whitewashed and lathe-turned legs of an old-fashioned communal table.

PROJECT ORANGE

Wine Rooms at Smiths of Smithfield, 2007, London / UK

Client : **Smiths** | Photography : **Gareth Gardner**

Smiths of Smithfield is the Grade II listed, four-story restaurant at the heart of Smithfield Market, London's only working meat market. Chef and owner John Torode approached Project Orange to remodel the first floor cocktail bar into a new casual dining room, including a private room with its own bar. The designers opened the space up to form a large democratic dining room with two discrete (and discreet) private rooms. The edge of the space is defined by a rustic timber wine wall that extends up to the ceiling and contains crates of special wine. The linear white marble bar is finished off with a polished brass foot rail and is designed so that customers may eat there, as well. The menu is written up on blackboards that are mounted within the wine wall. A new pine floor was also laid, lending warmth to the room while contrasting with the black oiled oak used for all the furniture and fixtures. The team designed a pair of freestanding screens and trestle tables and painted the private wine room in Suffolk Pink, a reference to whitewash made pink through the addition of bulls' blood, and also a wine.

STUDIO ILSE
Matsalen, 2007,
Stockholm / Sweden

Client: **Mathias Dahlgren Grand Hotel Stockholm** |
Design: **Studio Ilse (Ilse Crawford)** | Photography: **Åke E:son Lindman**

This hotel restaurant offers two varieties of dining experience designed by Ilse Crawford. The two-starred a la carte *"Matsalen"* (The Dining Room) is the more intimate and slow-moving service and reflects the character of cosmopolitan Swedish cooking. It seats 38 guests in a setting where the furnishings – recognizably Swedish and Scandinavian seating, tables, and lighting fill the room – extend the eating experience, which is based on the juxtaposition of creative cuisine and its traditional presentation.

PROJECT ORANGE

I-talia, 2009,
New Delhi / India

Client : **Apeejay Surrendra Park Hotels** |
Photography : **Ali Rangoonwala**

The design of the *I-Talia* eatery represents a collision of rustic simplicity and catwalk glamour. Set in a classical shopping center environment at Vasant Kunj in New Delhi, the interior concept drew on historic connections between India and Italy: Roman ships took advantage of monsoon winds to cross the Indian Ocean in order to trade spices, gems, and ivory for gold during the first century. Project Orange envisioned a dialogue between aromatic and exotic spices and the richness of gold and silver, seeing in it a narrative that ties the two countries together and shapes the look and feel of the restaurant. Customers are greeted by a gleaming polished brass totem that sits in front of the horizontally boarded curved oak wall. To the left is the café; a re-

laxed, simple room built up in white-painted brickwork with timber beams and a natural terracotta tiled floor. The private room eschews the other space's farmhouse rusticity and is instead decked out in understated luxury.

|[◦] JUXTAPOSITION → pp. 242–243

DESIGN RESEARCH STUDIO
Shoreditch House,
2007, London / UK

Client : **Shoreditch House** | Design : **Tom Dixon**

Design Research Studio and Tom Dixon designed the 14-room, 4000-square-meter private members club, *Shoreditch House,* on the top three floors of London's old Biscuit Factory. The private dining room is a luxe rendering of Soho House's "home away from home" aesthetic.

CONCRETE ARCHITECTURAL ASSOCIATES

Pearls & Caviar, 2008, Abu Dhabi / United Arab Emirates

Client: **Shangri La Hotel Abu Dhabi** | Project Team: **Rob Wagemans, Lisa Hassanzadeh, Sofie Ruytenberg, Erik van Dillen** | Photography: **Richard Thorn**

Pearls & Caviar is the Abu Dhabi Shangri-La Hotel's dining room. Concrete was asked to make a fish restaurant that was "a total art work" including the corporate identity (name, logo, menu, business cards, website, advertisement), the landscaping, interior, tableware, and the uniforms. In short, a design that would represent the new Arabian lifestyle, a luxury fusion of Occident and Orient, light and shadow, extroversion and introversion; celebrating both intimacy and the waterfront views. To concretize abstracted commonly used eastern forms and materials without losing their richness. They achieved this by replacing the traditional wealth of color associated with the region with either shades of black or shades of white, or both in combination with silver.

Dividing the restaurant into two themes, the designers created a terrace that articulates the pearl motif. The pearl areas are extroverted spaces composed completely in shades of white and silver with a large oriental carpet made of glass mosaic tiles in the same color scheme. A circular bar made of polished stainless steel with a bar top of white marble encircles the tower of the main terrace. The caviar section of the restaurant is an introverted, intimate, and appropriately windowless space dressed in shades of black and silver: The oriental carpet here is made of glass mosaic tiles in a black-silver color palette. This floor is divided into small chambers separated by ball chain curtains and side tables made of wenge. On top of them, Persian accessories are placed, which function as light diffusers.

|[I+] HIGH TECH. →p. 225

NATOMA ARCHITECTS
Conduit Restaurant,
2008, San Francisco / USA

Client : **Brian Spiers** |Design : **Stanley Saitowitz, Alan Tse** |
Photography : **Rien van Rijthoven**

Conduit's design in a ground floor commercial space beneath a new residential building was a quick-thinking response to the raw, low-ceilinged, and conduit-entangled interior that the designer was given to work with. To cover these pipes would have further diminished the size and presence of the space. Instead, even more conduits were layered over the existing ones to counteract and remediate the situation. The private dining room is a sheer glass box backed by a wall filled with wine racks and punctuated with the graphical vertical lines of, you guessed it, more conduits.

SHH
ARCHITECTS
Dion, 2007,
London / UK

Client: **Dion** | Design: **Neil Hogan, Addy Walcott** |
Photography: **Francesca Yorke and Morley von Sternberg**

A glamorous champagne bar set within an historic industrial building on West India Quay in London's Canary Wharf. The space includes a ground floor and lower-ground floor bar and restaurant space, as well as an outside semi-open and semi-tented terrace space, sponsored by Veuve Clicquot. Glowing golden doors slide across the length of the room to open the lounge or close it off for greater privacy.

MARCIO KOGAN

Forneria San Paolo, 2009,
São Paulo / Brazil

Author: **Marcio Kogan** | Co-authors: **Lair Reis, Diana Radomysler** |
Team: **Oswaldo Pessano, Renata Furlanetto Samanta Cafardo,
Suzana Glogowski, Carolina Castroviejo, Eduardo Glycerio,
Maria Cristina Motta Gabriel Kogan, Mariana Simas** |
Photography: **Rômulo Fialdini**

This restaurant, located in one of the city's upscale malls, has a minimalist interior enriched by a play of materials and transparencies. Warm, grainy wood wall panels and wooden lathes running in long stripes across the ceiling make the space elegant, cozy, and acoustically sound. The floor is composed of small colored stones, forming a mosaic. The kitchen opens onto the main dining area, separated from it by only a glass wall coated in a special pellicle that, depending on one's perspective, can appear milky sheer or transparent. This wall, which also carries a deep rectangular wooden frame through which diners may watch activities in the kitchen, creates a distinct relationship between kitchen and dining room, host and guest. Kogan used copper-colored pendant lights by Tom Dixon above the tables and arranged 15 George Nelson clocks, from the 50s and 60s, and re-edited by VITRA, chaotically across the wood-paneled walls, displaying the time in various time zones.

VIEW DESIGN STUDIO AND SHUBIN + DONALDSON

Bottega Louie,
2009, Los Angeles / USA

Design: **Keat Bollenbach** |
Photography: **Eric Richardson, Vam Y. K. Cheung**

A restaurant, gourmet market, florist, patisserie, café, and bar that celebrates empty space, bright natural light, and white tiles along with $1 cups of Lamill coffee. In a former Brooks Brothers flagship in remarkably uninviting downtown L.A., this place is inviting. The *Bottega* is an aromatic and old school mix of brass, Italian marble, tufted leather, tip-top service, and bright, airy space. The only decoration on Louie's 20-foot white walls, aside from generous glazing, are plaster cartouches copied from 14th-century Parisian residences, but the restaurant's hostess stands behind a gilded Louis XVI console table. Opulently exposed to the clientele, her position cultivates a special relationship between diner and staff from the very first moment that eye contact is made.

JOSEPH DIRAND
Hotel Habita, 2008,
Monterrey / Mexico
Client: **Hotel Habita Monterrey**

So austere and duotone a design, that you might be forgiven for thinking that the photos of the restaurant in *Hotel Habita* were shot in black and white. Dirand's stunning two-color interiors and terrace recuse themselves for the sake of the hotel's mind-blowing views of the Monterrey landscape and, in keeping with the rest of the property, as an expression of chic reserve. The reserve of the space is precisely the quality that – graciously, discreetly – gives the hotel guest or diner the privacy and freedom to relax (into work or into play) that is usually so lacking in a modern-day hotel and its eating space. Dirand ensures that there are no layers of frantic, purposeless, or invasive design between the guest and his personal experience of, in fact submersion into, this particular place, at this particular time.

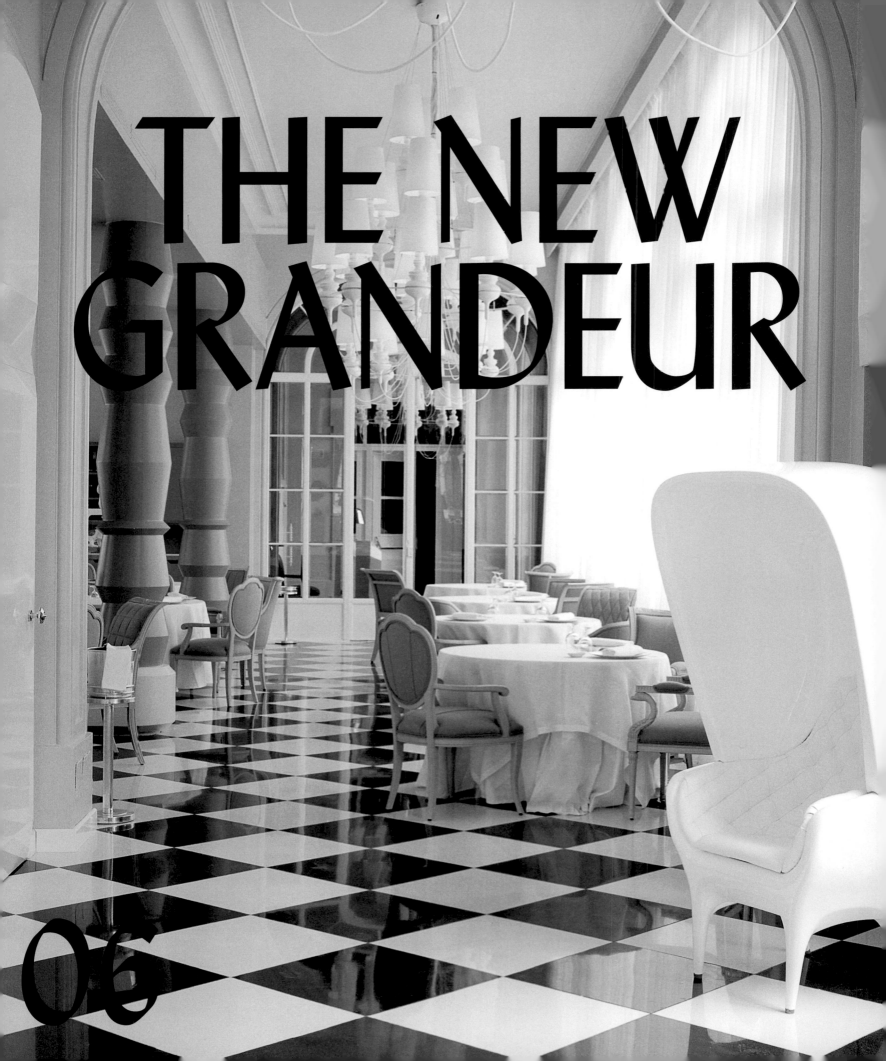

THE NEW GRANDEUR

06

Throughout history, grandeur has been signaled by the precious and the monumental. Today it sometimes takes less rigid, status-encrusted forms. At a time when luxury is available (in a watered-down way perhaps) to greater swarms of the population, how can a designer redefine it?

Today's exclusivity is about knowing the secrets and mapping the unmarked doors. <u>Christopher Tierney</u> remade a former Chinese take-out into a lush 18th-century boîte where the value is on rarity of ingredients, the bespoke, and on the personal experiences these

engender; on things that are no longer made or hard-to-find – whether it's cocktails, views, furnishings, or the restaurant, itself. At places like APOTHEKE, no one will be turned away who knows where to find the door and once inside, the pampering begins…

Grandeur is about contrasts as much as pampering: the deliciousness of eating and drinking well in the slums. Behind a vulgar, greasy-spoon exterior, guests are wrapped in opulence. The historic has become decadent in and of itself because its age and the authenticity of its materials and finishes (from cast iron pillars to bare brick walls) tell secret

stories. But age is more greatly appreciated when juxtaposed with the modern, or with modern elements that have the potential to become classics in their own right. <u>Jaime Hayon</u> played wittily with historical notions of luxury in LA TERRAZO DEL CASINO by perverting classical forms (running a column's fluting sideways) while maintaining them at a classical scale. Many eating space designers also recognize that views – from terraces, through windows – are tools of decadence as well because they frame the incomparable masterworks of either nature or man. In Stockholm's LE ROUGE, however, <u>Stylt Trampoli</u> found themselves without a window to work with, discovering instead that, as in the boudoir, artifice can prove as sublime as authenticity: they draped the walls with fabric and oil paintings to create a stage setting that became essential to the restaurant's rich flavor.

Finally, there's always the grandeur of having so much that anything can be thrown away: <u>Christian Liaigre's</u> BUDDAKAN exudes luxury in the form of a generous waste of the one thing that is most precious in New York City: space.

HAYON STUDIO
La Terraza del Casino,
2007, Madrid / Spain

Design: **Jaime Hayon** | Photography: **Nienke Klunder**

Madrid restaurant *La Terraza del Casino* was redesigned by Spaniard Jaime Hayon, who has exuberantly modernized its Versailles aesthetic by playing with materials, finishes, scale, and color. Hayon simplified classical forms, turning fluting on a column sideways, adding amber coatings to the glass on French doors, and draining the color from classic quilted armchairs, leaving much of the furniture white or blue-gray. The high-gloss checkered floor has blue checks instead of black and squares of monumental diameter, matched by the diamond pattern of an entirely mirrored wall. Smoothing out ornament to its minimum while still preserving it, Hayon's inventive, hybrid, and surreal environment is well-suited to chef Paco Roncero's innovative menus.

AUTOBAN
The House Café Istinye,
2007, Istanbul / Turkey

Design : **Seyhan Özdemir & Sefer Çaglar** | Photography : **Ali Bekman**

Since this was the first time that a *House Café* would be located away from the heart of Istanbul, Autoban wanted to bring a bit of the city into the interior. The wall-less and columnless metal train station and clock tower "frames" were just the ticket to create the suggestion of a city square. This is the largest eatery in the chain, boasting a seating capacity of 200, and is appropriately bigger in scale and personality. The whole atmosphere is fascinating with the latest special designs accompanying the furniture classics of *The House Cafés*. The space was just like a city square with no surrounding walls or columns. Natural daylight penetrates the wireframe city from the mall's roof, pouring over patrons seated at the café's marble tables and making for a comfortable, yet spectacular, experience.

AUTOBAN
Kitchenette Bebek,
2008, Istanbul / Turkey

Client **Istanbul Doors** | Design **Seyhan Özdemir & Sefer Çaglar** |
Photography : **Ali Bekman**

Spread over three floors, the *Kitchenette*
branch in Bebek introduces two fresh concepts
on its upper floors. Baronette, on the second floor,
is the lounge area where guests sip cocktails as a
pre-club activity. The Library Room on the third
floor, is designed in the manner of an old world
gentleman's club and accompanied by a tapas bar.
Tufted leather sofas, generous mullioned windows, and admirable art deco pressed-tin ceiling
details create a first class experience.

BLACKSHEEP
St. Germain, 2006,
London / UK

Client : **Neil Walkington** | Photography : **Edmund Sumner**

Blacksheep sought to recreate the ambiance of New York's finest bars and restaurants in London's Farringdon district. While they created an understated and simple interior where the food and drink could take center stage, the light-filled, geometric, and monochrome concept has the self-assurance and grand classicism of a Parisian brasserie. Being tall always helps: the ground floor bar and restaurant area is a naturally dramatic double-height space with large windows both at the street and opposite rear side. Certain of its authenticity, original and honest materials and finishes have been kept; from the cast iron supporting pillars to bare brick walls (enhanced and made more contemporary by being sprayed in matte cream paint). Blacksheep's interior concept adds layers of interest, from textured, black and white vertically-striped paper for the wall opposite the bar, to oversized backlit angled mirrors to encourage restaurant activity at both ends of the dining area.

CHRISTOPHER TIERNEY

Apotheke, 2008,
New York / USA

Client : **New York City Cocktail Culture and Social Premium** |
Photography : **Matthias Gaggl**

No one will be turned away at the door, if only they can find it. Behind a garish red plastic storefront that once marked the Golden Flower Restaurant, entering *Apotheke* from the elbow of a quiet, trash-strewn Chinatown side street is like falling through the back of the wardrobe into Narnia. Tierney has remade a former Chinese take-out into a luxe 18th-century, royal Austrian "apothecary," where patrons take the cure in the form of more than 250 baroque cocktails blended from rare botanicals, custom-infused liquors, and other house-made elixirs. The liquids menu highlights ingredients like opium leaves, absinthe, habanero, and espresso and lists remedies by category: everything from "stress relievers" and "painkillers" to "aphrodisiacs" and "euphoric enhancers." "Therapeutic treatments" use gin as their base, since the spirit is known to affect the frontal lobe of the brain where speech, emotions, and reason originate. In white jackets, skilled bartenders work behind a heavy, nearly room-length internally illuminated marble bar. The intimate grandeur of the darkened room is framed with an uneven parquet wood floor, overstuffed Victorian sofas and armchairs, and an elaborately painted pressed-tin ceiling. The faded and comforting Old World atmosphere should remind all "patients" that no matter how jaded they may feel with their cosmopolitan lives, of course, we have nothing if we don't have our health.

CLAESSON KOIVISTO RUNE

Operakällaren, 2005,
Stockholm / Sweden

Client : **Nobis AB, through Alessandro Catenacci** |
Design : **Claesson Koivisto Rune / Mårten Claesson, Eero
Koivisto, Ola Rune, Deta Gemzell, Patrick Coan, Olivia Herms**
| Mr. **Åke E:son Lindman** | FurnitureManufacturers, bespoke solutions :
**Boffi, Living Divani, Fornasarig, Kasthall, Italamp, Örsjö
Lighting** | Additional Furniture Manufacturers : **De Vecchi, Almedahls,
Maharam**

Operakällaren (Swedish for "Opera Cellar"), which opened in 1787 in Stockholm's Royal Opera House, has long been a Swedish institution and a culinary destination; ornately decorated interiors dating from 1895 are, wisely, protected as a cultural heritage. CKR's gentle approach to the renovation updated and preserved the restaurant, with the hope that a new generation of guests and long-time regulars will both feel at ease in the space. "Is there such a thing as timeless elegance? And if so, what does it look like?" the designers asked themselves. In response, they chose a metaphor: the pinstriped suit. These subtle sartorial lines have been a steadfast signal of quality and sophistication and remained fashionable through the manifold sea of changes in fashion. The new interior connects to the idea, both metaphorically and literally, while creating contrast between modern furniture and materials and the very classical rooms, a contrast that adds both vitality and grandeur, resulting in a new interior with a preserved atmosphere. The designers stripped away musty velvet curtains and added technical lighting to showcase fine old woodwork and existing murals. The strongest architectural component is a series of free-standing, giant, angled mirrors that begin at the entrance, continue through a wide corridor to the dining hall, and into the new veranda bar. The mirrors are made of unexpected gold-tinted mirror glass, laminated with a newly developed high-tech film. The film is made in such a way as to affect the area of vision that perceives reflected images, narrowing the field of reflection by blurring what is around it. In the middle of each mirror is a horizontal division where the film's reflective effect is inverted. This means that patrons never see the reflection of their own faces. And the mirrors' slight backward cant also highlights the richly embellished ceiling. In a veranda bar that had been added to the building in the 1960s, KCR raised the floor to match that of the dining hall and clear the windows of fussy panels, brass bars, and unnecessary curtains to reveal a decadent view of historic central Stockholm, including the Royal Palace.

IDING INTERIOR DESIGN
Stanislavski, 2009,
Amsterdam /
the Netherlands

Client : **Amsterdam Village Company** | Photography : **Teo Krijgsman**

Running along the face of Amsterdam's City Theater, the *Stanislavski* is monumental in scale and in the timeless richness of its regal finishes. But within this stately environment, it also offers creature comforts and the comfort of choice, with all sorts of places to sit, to match each mood or group: at high tables alongside the bar, at an intimate spot on one of the many inviting couches, at a seat at the tall "kitchen table," or on the terrace outside with views of the city center. IDING opened and reconnected the numerous parti-tioned spaces in the theater during the building process to create this sense of epic exposure to the outside world and to its interiors; by adding furnishings that are warm, comfy, and human-scaled.Simultaneously they made it cozy, a surprising accomplishment.

ROMAN & WILLIAMS

Brasserie 44, Royalton Hotel, 2007, New York / USA

Client : **John MacDonald; Morgans Hotel Group** |
Photography : **Nikolas Koenig**

Robin Standefer and Stephen Alesch of Roman & Williams created a gentleman's playground in the lobby of the Royalton Hotel and in the *Brasserie 44* behind it. It is earthy, armored with thick green leather wall panels and cushioned with quilted leather couches, while the cool dimness is made into a design element and a refuge as well. But it is also of the sea, with woven rope arches dividing the dining booths, teak wood, and globe lanterns that remind visitors of a moonrise seen from the rigging of a ship.

DAVID COLLINS STUDIO

Bob Bob Ricard Restaurant,
2008, London / UK

Client: **Private Owner** | Photography: **Richard Howarth**

To create a space for "dining" that would work throughout the day and into the evening, David Collins used images that evoke the golden age of travel, drawing heavily on inspiration from the late 19th- and early 20th-century Paris to Istanbul Orient Express passenger train. Aided by its whiff of intrigue and opulence, Collins made bold use of patterns, prints, and luxe fabrics and finishes to shape a dining destination that feels sophisticated at any time of the day or night.

TADAO ANDO
Morimoto, 2006,
New York / USA

Client : **Starr Restaurant Organization** | New York Project Architect :
Stephanie Goto / Goto Design Group | Photography : **Richard Pare**

Manhattan's *Morimoto* serves Japanese food in a theme park of architectural and industrial design flourishes. *Morimoto's* tactility and well-considered material palette suggest that Osaka-based Ando has had a hand in its creation. "Materiality is really important here," says the project's creative director and producer, Stephanie Goto of Goto Design Group. "You're always looking at something new." The vast, two-story interior is distinguished by Ando's signature unfinished concrete walls and its dramatic curtain, an undulating gray-white fabric hardened with fiberglass and hung on heavy chains beneath the existing ceiling. Elsewhere, the architects used resin, woods, and even water bottles to build the space: A 9-ton light sculpture made from more than 17,000 Ty Nant water bottles greets diners at the front door. It was designed by Ross Lovegrove, who designed much of the varied seating for the restaurant, including a squishy foam chair that could be mistaken for a chunk cleaved from one of Ando's concrete walls.

CHRISTIAN LIAIGRE
Buddakan, 2006,
New York / USA

Client : **Starr Restaurant Organization** | New York Project Architect :
Stephanie Goto / Goto Design Group Photography : **David Joseph**

What unexpected contradictions haven't been brought together in this exalted space? In a vast series of cavernous black chambers, Liaigre thumbs his nose at Manhattan's typical claustrophobic spatial squeeze. His restaurant exudes luxury in the form of a generous and strategic waste of what is most precious in New York City: space. Super-high ceilings create an airy void above a long banquet table at the heart of the jewel-box interiors. Eastern and western paintings and tapestries are blown up to twice their size on walls while carved, lacquered screens filigree the wood-paneled walls. In the cellar space, a bar is wallpapered with the spines of the gilded leather volumes of a library, across the way Lascaux-like wall drawings, saturated colors, glossy surfaces, and oversized Asian urns dwarf diners while also allowing them to feel coddled.

BURNS
DESIGN LIMITED
21212, 2009,
Edinburgh / Scotland
Client: **Rrock Limited** | Photography: **Gareth Easton**

Round chesterfield-like booths, enlarged details from Old Master paintings, curtained walls, and an ornately paneled ceiling encourage a unique and dramatic dining experience in an otherwise merely stately Georgian townhouse in Edinburgh. Like the space, the modern French cuisine has a gourmet twist.

PIET BOON STUDIO
Hof van Saksen, 2007, Nooitgedacht / the Netherlands

Client **Hof van Saksen Holiday Resort** | Photography: **Kees Hageman** | Styling: **Rianne Landstra**

Piet Boon designed the interior of this 10,000-square-meter public building at a popular holiday resort, as well as the interiors of its farmhouse cottages, making each space an experience in itself. The campus also includes four restaurants, ranging from an exclusive à la carte dining room to a self-service lunchroom that make contemporary references to the region's rural culture while emphasizing a highbrow restfulness: the walls are muted in white plaster to provide a background for art and photography, while materials such as oak (in the lively form of staggered angled walls) and high-quality natural fabrics mix amiably with clean-lined furnishings. In the grand café, dark tints make the space feel intimate and warmly enticing.

JAGDFELD DESIGN
MA – Tim Raue,
2008, Berlin / Germany

Client : **Tim Raue** | Design : **Anne Maria Jagdfeld** |
Photography : **Reto Guntli** | Copyright : **amj design**

Ma, which means horse in Chinese, suits this pinpoint-illuminated Asia-inspired restaurant, whose centerpiece, along with lauded chef, Tim Raue, is a proud Han-dynasty stone horse showcased in a vast museum box. Designed by Anne Maria Jagdfeld, the creative mind behind other luxe locations such as China Club, it is an interior rich with lush materials like wenge, slate, bronze, jade, and cashmere. Ma's millennia-old clay horse statue dates from the third century B.C. and, at 1.43 meters, towers over the middle of the room. The spot-on light design also emphasizes a hand-made bronze portal, high glass walls that front a vertical garden in the inner courtyard, and a small waterscape that creates a tranquil background. The open kitchen is visible from the dining room through a large window and thus becomes an integral component of the overall interior design.

STYLT TRAMPOLI AB

Le Rouge, 2007,
Stockholm / Sweden

Client : **F12 Group** | Photography : **Erik Nissen Johansen**

As one might expect of a restaurant dubbed *Le Rouge,* this is a lively, warm, and luxurious setting. The interior is reminiscent of a French supper club from the turn of the 19th century, like the Moulin Rouge, and marked by vibrant colors, heavy textiles, and plenty of period detail. Three things in particular characterize the food at *Le Rouge:* personality, tradition, and warmth, all of which exist in spades in the softly draped, sexily crimson dining room. Working without any openings to the outside, Stylt Trampoli designers instead hung ornately framed oil paintings in Louvre-like profusion over the ceiling instead of the walls. "There is always a challenge in designing spaces without windows," says a *Le Rouge* designer. "Covering the ceiling with fabrics while pleasing the fire authorities was tricky. Without daylight it became more a set decoration than interior design."

JUAN & BORJA INFANTE
Negro de Anglona, 2006,
Madrid / Spain

Interior Design : **Luis Galliussi** | **Photography :** **Luis Hevia**

Ironically, this Madrid cellar cultivates the sophistication of a palace. Its palatial décor with a self-assured patrician aesthetic is the work of architect and interior designer Luis Galliussi and the brothers Juan & Borja Infante, the second generation of a well-known Madrid hospitality group, which was also responsible for Samarkanda, La Leyenda, Berlin Cabaret, and Pizza Jardin. The space is made unique through the creation of a long narrow gallery of black and white photographs of palace scenarios and, in the foyer, richly patterned floor-to-ceiling wall hangings. Surprisingly, this fine-dining setting (immaculate white linen tablecloths, generous cloche wine glasses, subdued black walls) flaunts a reasonably priced Mediterranean-Oriental fusion menu.

HIGH-TECH

07

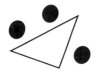
Eating spaces infused with technology may be functionally high-tech or aesthetically so. At the tail end of the digital revolution, designers are bored with their end-of-the-millennium neglect of the handmade in favor of all things virtual and have begun

to create hybrid environments that bring craft and computer together. Michael Young does this in Hong Kong's PISSARRO where he brings hand-blown glass and hand-folded paper walls together with industrial processes and computer-controlled production. Conspicuously techie restaurants, like London's INAMO, may have menus projected in living color over each guest's place-setting and tables that can be altered to suit the mood of the party. Or, like BANQ in Boston, they may have

layers of geometrical architecture that has been constructed from advanced

production processes like CNC milling. Lehanneur turned "technology" on its head in FLOOD by using a low-tech – dare we say primitive? – tool (air-filtering algae) to accomplish something (maintain, measure and indicate air quality) that might seem a bit sci-fi to a civilian. Other spaces look gorgeously apocalyptic – framed by conduits or populated with space pods – or serenely au naturale – diners find themselves outdoors when they walk inside – precisely because designers were limited by windowless sites or equally blind clients. And for this we are grateful.

BLACKSHEEP
Inamo, 2008, London / UK

Graphics : **Helen Gilbert / Blacksheep** | Photography : **Francesca Yorke**

Blacksheep designed an Asian-fusion restaurant featuring interactive dining, with colorful menus projected onto tabletops, allowing diners to order food and beverages, change the ambiance of their individual table, play games or even order up local information and services (such as booking a cab). The interior had to have a strong identity, neither overwhelming nor being overwhelmed by the technology at its heart. "We created a concept based around the keywords: warmth, vibrancy, charm, and theater," explains Blacksheep Director Tim Mutton. "It was important to balance out the restaurant's technological aspects by creating a sensuous, social space with a strong personality."

SIMON HEIJDENS

Espresso Bar Boijmans van Beuningen, 2008, Rotterdam / the Netherlands

Client : **Boijmans van Beuningen Museum Rotterdam |**
Photography: **Simon Heijdens**

Heijdens emphasizes, and pays respect to, the café table as a social surface around which neighbors come together to share the news of the day. Here, he imagines it – literally – as a sign of its times, a bearer of fleeting information: a stream of newspaper headlines, magazine articles, flyers, and packaging. Moreover, where the museum curates its art, the *Espresso Bar* curates its visitors. A specifically developed optical software reads and interprets all the words that pass the table surface on newspaper headlines, magazine articles, flyers, and packaging, and distills those words to a central database. The flat text is then converted into a weave that continuously grows over days and weeks, fed by the words that pass the table. Word by word, the weave grows in a spiral onto the ceiling above each of the 16 tables, and becomes a slowly expanding legible archive that bears the history of the use of the table. By not only carrying, but also reading and interpreting that information, the table becomes a document of its consumption, digestion, and use and an archive of current, local culture.

200

BLUARCH
Central Lounge and Sushi Bar,
2008, New York / USA

Client : **Charlie and Jack Trantides** | Design : **Antonio Di Oronzo** |
Photography : **SGM Photography**

Central Lounge and Sushi Bar is a supper club that offers the indulgent environment of a lounge and the sensual experience of eating sushi in a rich and eclectic space. The venue has two bars, one rectangular and one circular, both armored in tufted white upholstery and topped with slabs of back-lit onyx. Above the rectangular bar, five walnut shelters curve at different heights to create a refined sense of intimacy. Each shelter has a cut-out area revealing a black mirror and a Swarovski crystal sconce. The circular section of the restaurant is crowned by a mezzanine which opens to double height and is topped with froths of ivy and LED lights. The perimeter of this area is delineated by a round banquette above which round upholstered panels in different sizes line the walls. "The experience was unique," designer Antonio di Oronzo admits, "in that I was creating a venue for Japanese food without implementing the usual Japanese design language."

ELECTRIC DREAMS

Pleasant Bar, 2007,
Stockholm / Sweden

Client : **Carl-Johan Tingström/ Daniel Tingström** |
Graphics : **Dizel&Sate** | Photography : **Fredrik Sweger**

Pleasant Bar used to look decidedly un-pleasant. It was a dive with smoke-stained walls, yet the old owner doesn't think much of the new design. "Every time we run into him," says one of the designers, "he clenches his fist and starts yelling, "What have you done to my beautiful bar!! What a disgrace! You two should be ashamed of yourselves!!" But the new interior reminds its new owner of the place he finds most beautiful the world over: Tobago's Pleasant Prospect, which is evoked by "a fragmented fever dream" pictured across one wall, in which a city meets an enchanted forest filled with Tobago-nian flora and fauna. The endless mirror ball ceiling allows customers to spy on each other in the intimate, 65-square-meter space, while even the wall framing the bar forms a graphic element and serves as a bottle stand, DJ booth, and an area for narrow one-cocktail-only tables. Seating consists of a mix of vintage chairs that were given unity when coated with glossy black lacquer. The graphics, a series of exterior glass illustra-tions, and the urban forest wallpaper were made by Dizel & Sate. Different excerpts from the wall illustration top each backlit glass table. Joel De-germark's Cluster Lamps for Moooi hang above each table, each kitted out with a different set of light bulbs. The mirror walls and ceiling in the restrooms give the illusion of infinity and create a kaleidoscopic effect, while strands of fiber-op-tic threads are reflected in the bathroom ceilings and walls, creating an endless sea of illuminated grass. It seems both appropriate and pleasant that the bar offers only five tables for eating and drinking, but plenty of room to dance.

JOHANNES TORPE

Subu Restaurant,
2007, Beijing / China

Client : **South Beauty Group**

Torpe rooted his design in traditional Chinese culture, while working to create an environment wholly new to the country. "We wanted to nail an airport feeling and make the place visible from the whole mall," the designer explains, "So we created five arches over the eating area to attract people." The arches are dramatic, but the cocoons are Torpe's 21ˢᵗ-century rendition of the classic Chinese private dining room. These glossy pods both update and increase the intimacy of the conventional private booth. *Subu* is truly a bespoke space: everything from furniture to tableware was designed for it. "In fact," says Torpe, "this is not an interior design; this is one big industrial design."

SERIE
ARCHITECTS
Blue Frog Acoustic Lounge &
Studios, 2007, Mumbai / India

Client: **Blue Frog Media Pvt. Ltd** | Photography: **Fram Petit**

Serie converted a large industrial warehouse in the old mill district of Mumbai into a complex housing sound recording studios and an acoustic lounge. The challenge lay in collapsing theater, restaurant, bar, and club into an open warehouse whilst maintaining the functional characteristics of each type of space. The architect's solution was to organize the space in a cellular fashion, composed of circles of varying sizes in plan and approximating a horseshoe configuration. The cylinders were extruded to different heights to create tiered seating booths that distribute the gaze of diners and standing patrons across staggered levels, which, amphitheater-like, increase in height away from the stage. These booths seat between four to ten people and are arranged around a void that can either double as a potential 360° stage or accommodate standing pa-

trons, bringing them closer to the main stage to create an intimate viewing experience. The mahogany paneled booths not only maintain uninterrupted views to the stage, but also a constant distance between diners, irrespective of how crowded the lounge gets. The undulating height of the booths is also gently modulated by a glowing acrylic resin surface, which unifies the disparate zones and gives the architecture a high profile even in the midst of a state–of–the–art sound and light show.

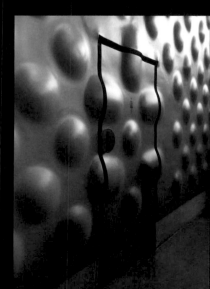

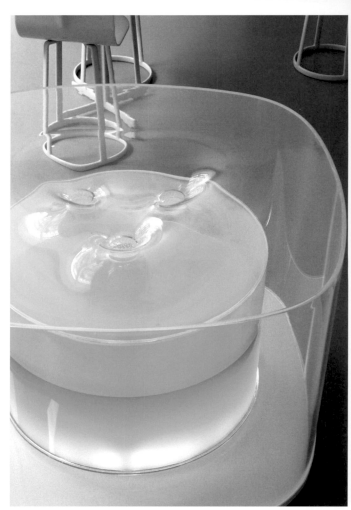

MATHIEU LEHANNEUR
Flood, 2007, Paris / France

Client | **Flood** | Photography | **Cyril Afsa**

Inspired by science and engineering, designer Mathieu Lehanneur's interior and furniture for Paris restaurant *Flood* attempt to match the quality of the international food with the quality of its air. To filter the interior's air, Lehanneur placed an aquarium in the center of each section of the dining room containing over 100 liters of Spirulina platensis, or micro-algae. Through photosynthesis, the algae generates pure oxygen. He designed bespoke furniture based on the notion of flooding by dip-coating the PVC furniture. He also created his own way to measure and indicate the quality of the oxygen-enriched air via the blown-glass pendant lamps.

[A]

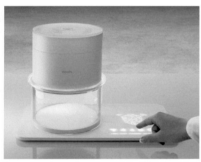

[B]

[C]

[D]

[E]

PHILIPS DESIGN
Philips Design Probe FOOD,
2009, the Netherlands

Client: **Philips Design**

Philips's FOOD Probes take a provocative and unconventional look at areas that could have a profound effect on the way we eat and source our food 15 to 20 years from now. These investigations examined the possible consequences of various long-range social trends relating to food. This involved tracking and interpreting issues like the shift in emphasis from curative to preventive medicine, the growth in popularity of organic produce, the implications of genetic modification, land use patterns in growing what we eat, the threat of serious food shortages, and rising prices. The result was the addition to Philips's ongoing Design Probes program of three new concepts: *Diagnostic Kitchen, Food Creation* and *Home Farming.*

[A] – Diagnostic Kitchen Concept: Diagnostic Kitchen allows users to assess and follow their optimum eating regimen. By using the nutrition monitor, consisting of a scanning "wand" and swallowable sensor, users can determine exactly what and how much to eat to achieve their maximum digestive health at that moment in time.

[B-E] – Food Creation Concept: Food Creation takes its cues from the "molecular gastronomists," the chefs who deconstruct food and then reassemble it in surprising ways. The food printer would accept various edible ingredients and then combine and "print" them in the desired shape and consistency, like the stereolithographic printers that create 3-D representations of product concepts.

[F] – Home Farming Concept: Home Farming explores growing at least part of one's daily calorific requirements at home. This biosphere home-farm has been designed to occupy a minimum of floor space by stacking its various mini-ecosystems on top of each other. This vertical farm contains fish, crustaceans, algae, and edible plants; all interdependent and in balance with each other and includes systems for water filtration, recycling of nutrients, and optimum use of sunlight.

DESIGN SPIRITS CO., LTD.

Beijing Noodle No. 9,
2009, Las Vegas / USA

Client : **Caesars Palace** | Design : **Yuhkichi Kawai** |
Photography : **Barry Johnson**

A modern Chinese restaurant located within a gargantuan casino hotel with more than 3,300 rooms in Las Vegas. Since the restaurant is adjacent to the casino, the excitement, gaming machine sounds, and neon lights overflow into it contagiously. In general, a space usually consists of various interior elements, materials, products, and patterns placed appropriately. Instead, *Noodle No. 9* takes advantage of the site's lack of support columns to dictate a single pattern throughout the space. This approach generates a simultaneously minimal and decorative atmosphere that engenders tranquility without becoming dull. DSC created a surreal environment that balances opposites precisely, providing not only a respite from, but an extension of the casino. The design applies a single arabesque pattern that is repeated ad infinitum throughout the entire space. Beyond the sparkling aquarium tanks, in the deepest part of the restaurant, the architect's double-wall design features filigreed layers, consisting of one woodland-patterned steel decorative surface above a painted similarly patterned solid back, with glossy finish. This creates a cocooned feeling, as the wall rises into the ceiling. By placing LED indirect lights between the layers, the arabesques produce striking shadows that play against the restaurant's bright surfaces.

213

MICHAEL YOUNG
Pissarro Dining,
2008, Hong Kong / China

Concept and Execution : **Michael Young** | Interiors Furniture Design : **Michael Young** | Lighting Design : **Michael Young** | Design Engineering : **Ken O'Rourke** | Architectural Lighting : **Anlighten Design Studio** | Project Architect : **Sebastian Saint Jean** | Accupunto Specialist Paper Wall Finishing : **Michael Young Interiors** | Photography : **Harlim Djauhar Winata**

In the center of Hong Kong's nightlife district, British transplant, Michael Young, drew on recent experiments with craft and industrial processes for Artek and others to design a 1600-square-foot contemporary French restaurant. "I adore eating out and wanted to design a place that gave the comfort of a classic interior, but in contemporary terms," the designer explains. To create the front door, the team CNC-milled panels of aluminum anodized in specially created colors. 3M provided the wall and ceiling finishes, especially golden Di-Noc, an imitation wood veneer used in the auto industry during the 1940s and 50s, which helped generate depth and plane in an interior that was problematically thin. Having spent a couple of years developing techniques in paper-folding with local craftsmen to create furniture, Young decided to clad the walls using this same process. French impressionist artist Camille Pissarro, for whom the restaurant is named, experimented with pointillism in his later years. As he was celebrated for his skies, Young abstracted one of his skies digitally and duplicated it in a panel that contains 26,400 pieces of paper (the interior includes a total of over

300,000 pieces of paper). For seating, the studio made a special edition of Young's teak and leather Coen chair and a matching CNC-milled table. To break up the strong lines and industrial aspects of the interior, the designer handblew his own lighting in a small village workshop on Mount Fuji. The project is remarkable for its seamless union of traditional craft and technology-driven processes.

215

GRAFT

Gingko Bacchus Restaurant, 2009, Chengdu / China

Client : **Gingko Restaurant Management Corporation** | Still Life Exposed Works : **Kevin Best** | Photography : **Golf Tattler: Lai Xuzhu Oak Taylor Smith**

It may not have been the big bang, but the starting point for Graft's *Gingko Bacchus* interior was empty black space. The designers envisioned the public spaces of this 1200-square-meter restaurant as a stream along which patrons may float. This fourth-floor stream – whose flow is suggested by an undulating wood ceiling and the stainless steel intarsia of the floor – is accessed via a bank of elevators. Eight private dining rooms are arranged along it like boulders along a stream, each color-coded and themed by foods. Each private room features a bespoke wallpaper illustrated with carrots, mushrooms, walnuts, broccoli, beans, chilies, or artichokes. Floating from room to room, passersby experience a gentle shift from green to red along the color spectrum. In each chamber, blown-up photographic interpretations of traditional Dutch still life paintings are displayed at the full size of the wall, placed behind one-way mirrors and equipped with a time-controlled lighting system, so that specific sections of the images come into view and fade over time. The entire corridor is illuminated in slow motion, leaving, once the light fades, only the reflection of the viewer in the mirrored glass. The dining rooms are each hung with a pixelated abstraction of an historical painting of Bacchus, the god of wine. Through the laser cut pixels, the illuminated background of the vegetable wallpapers and Arcadian landscapes are visible while, on the ceiling above, the foreground and background of the painting is then reversed. The erotic subtext of these works is suggested in custom-designed counters, tables, and sofas, which are each composed of a pair of elements in various positions of embrace. Throughout the restaurant, an abundance of dark, tinted mirrors and reflective surfaces are used to create surreal extensions of the interior and disorient guests. Graft's graphic design ranged from the wallpapers to menus, amplifying the atmosphere of seduction, desire, and pursuit (if not the actual possession) of pleasure at every turn.

FRANK SPINDLER, JESKO KLATT

Spindler & Klatt, 2005,
Berlin / Germany

Client : **25+** | Photography : **www.diephotodesigner.de**

This lounge restaurant and nightclub beside the Spree River in Kreuzberg, a formerly industrial area of Berlin, is divided into a 1055-square-meter indoor area and 600-square-meter terrace dotted with futons. The former warehouse's generosity of scale – with 10-meter ceilings – determines the character of the nightspot. Three huge movable walls connect or close off the two zones. Big futon lounges, made from dark wood and piled with cream-colored pillows, are distributed around the dancing and lounge area. Far Asian antiques and Buddha statues give the impression of 1920s Shanghai. The 6-meter-wide terrace, made from cobbles common to the neighborhood, offers a fantastic view to the Oberbaumbrücke, Fernsehturm, and the Berlin Wall Gallery. The culinary concepts are based around the tenants of Zen and prepared in an open kitchen. In summertime, the lounge is open-air and is, at night, turned into a moody nightclub glowing with colored light and large videos projected through and onto large mobile gauze curtains. Every three months, Frank Spindler and Jesko Klatt plan to refresh the interior design throughout but the original concept will remain: without changing location, *Spindler & Klatt* guests can go from an Asian-European fusion dinner to a night of clubbing.

3DELUXE

Silk Bed Restaurant,
2004, Frankfurt
on the Main / Germany

Client : **Mario Lohninger, Cocoon Club** |
Photography : **Holger Uhlmann, Thomas Schauer**

In *Silk,* 3deluxe elevates eating and drinking to the level of an artistic ceremony based on Asian and other ancient eating rituals. Guests enter an atmospheric reception room, where they remove their shoes and put on tatami sandals. This Asian ritual emphasizes the private atmosphere of this exclusive restaurant, and signals to guests that they are about to have an unusual gastronomic experience. From the entrance, visitors are led to one of eight large white couch areas separated from each other by gauze curtains. Each of the upholstered units has room for up to nine persons to recline or sit. Food and drink are served on fine glass trays, and can be placed in channels flush in the beds and surrounding arm rests. The predominantly white surfaces of furnishings, walls, and ceiling are constantly washed in changing light, along with the double-layered white gauze and, between the gauze layers, filigreed metal ornaments that offer another layer of sensual distraction.

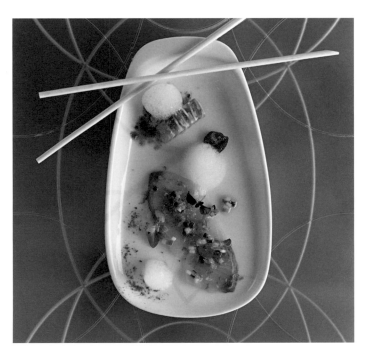

3DELUXE
Micro Fine Dining Restaurant,
2004, Frankfurt
on the Main / Germany

Client : **Mario Lohninger, Cocoon Club** |
Photography : **Holger Uhlmann, Thomas Schauer**

This 319-square-meter space consists of a restaurant, bar and lounge area, and an event space which doubles as the weekend's dance floor. Its cubic furnishings are made of dark woods, teak, and bamboo, but light plays a big role in 3Deluxe's design. A matrix of silver strings made of a couple thousand glass fibers that hang from the ceiling, nearly filling the room. This net is used as a three-dimensional object on which to screen video projections that are synchronized to pulse in time with the DJ'ed music. Eleven tables set for eight guests each can be divided by the matrix into smaller sections so views of the room and dining niches can be dynamically reconfigured each evening. A virtual chimney fire casts light and shadows onto the bamboo table surfaces. An even better show, however, can be seen along the edges of *Micro's* show kitchen, which offers a view of Michelin-starred chef Mario Lohninger and his team as they prepare dishes.

DESIGN SPIRITS CO., LTD.
Food LOuVER,
2007, Jakarta / Indonesia

Client : **Grand Indonesia** | Photography : **Infomedia Indonesia**

This unusually beautiful food court in a Jakarta shopping mall is an expression of Indonesian ethnicity, while its minimalism is simultaneously international. *Food LOuVER* is embellished with a single textural skin: simple wooden louvers as walls, seating, and partitions. While the louver is a minimal and modern material, the designer also used an array of natural materials native to Indonesia, such as a bark, grass, plants, bamboo, and wood, applying these to the surface of the louver. In one space the wood is bare, in another it is "garnished" with greenery and painted white. The food shops are ranged between the glassed outer walls of the mall and a middle corridor, allowing clients to enjoy the views outside.

224

|[+] OPEN & SHUT → p. 156

NATOMA ARCHITECTS
Conduit Restaurant,
2008, San Francisco / USA

Client: **Brian Spiers** | Design: **Stanley Saitowitz, Alan Tse** |
Photography: **Rien van Rijthoven**

Conduit's design emerged from the circumstances in which the site was found. A ground floor commercial space in a new residential building, the raw interior had a low ceiling and a tangled maze of plumbing, sprinkler, and electrical conduits serving the apartments above. To cover these pipes would have further diminished the size and presence of the space. Instead, even more conduits were layered over the existing ones to counteract and remediate the situation. The design, then, inspired the name. In the dining room, a series of conduit screens in galvanized steel or copper color divide the tables and, stacked, create an open bar. At the end of the room, another bar frames the open kitchen, providing a well-lit stage for the cooks and front row seats for the barflies.

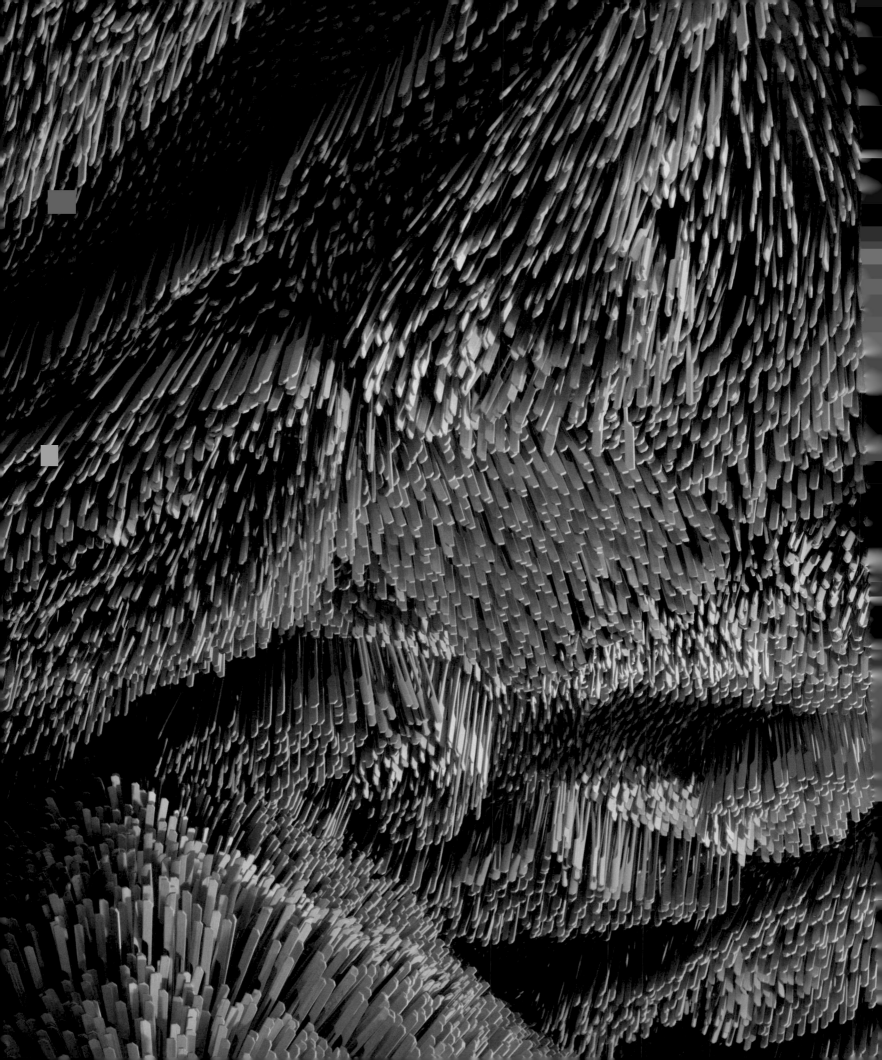

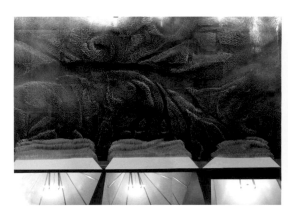

LEWIS. TSURUMAKI. LEWIS ARCHITECTS

Tides Restaurant, 2005, New York / USA

Client: **Steven Yee** | Photography: **Michael Moran**

At 39 square meters, the Lower East Side seafood restaurant *Tides* had room for two booths and five snuggly two-person tables – 20 guests make a full house. Nonetheless, the designers managed to conjure a sense of space where in fact there was none at all. Though LTL's exquisite experiment with various permutations of architectural bamboo has been swept away on the low ebb of the global economy, it has raised the bar on what can be accomplished with a wooden skewer. The ceiling was sown with over 110,000 bamboo skewers stuck (and welbonded) into a back-lit acoustical foam to produce a topographical effect that evoked sea grass. Walls and banquettes were made from blond and caramelized bamboo; bamboo ply lined with acrylic served for tables. LTL custom-made seven triangular sconces from a sanded sandwich of acrylic slices. Additional lighting inside the drop ceiling gave the tidepool-size dining room the dim glow of a kelp forest. The ceiling and canopies above the booths were the coup-de-grace, however: It took two people two weeks to install the deep shag of skewers that eddied over them. "We were up to 120,000 skewers," says architect Paul Lewis. "We decided we had to stop there."

OFFICE DA
Banq, 2008, Boston / USA

Project Design : **Nader Tehrani, Monica Ponce de Leon** | Principal in Charge : **Nader Tehrani** | Project Architect : **Dan Gallagher** | Project Coordinators : **Catie Newell, Brandon Clifford** | Project Team : **Harry Lowd, Richard Lee, Lisa Huang, Remon Alberts, Janghwan Cheon, Jumanah Jamal, Aishah Al Sager** | Contractor : **Homeland Builders** | Structural Consulting Engineer : **Simpson Gumpertz & Heger Inc. MEP** | Consulting Engineer : **Wozny/Barbar & Associates, Inc.** | Lighting Consultant : **Collaborative Lighting** | Acoustical Consultant : **Acentech** | Kitchen Consultant : **TriMark USA, Inc.** | Building Code Consultant : **Hal Cutler** | Photography : **John Horner**

Located in the old Penny Savings Bank, *Banq* is divided into two segments: the front bar area that runs along Washington Street and the larger hall behind it, which serves as the dining room. To keep the restaurant floor flexible and hide services at the ceiling, dA developed a striated wood-slat system that conceals the view of the mechanical, plumbing, and lighting systems, while offering a virtual canopy under which to dine. The geometry of the wooden slats conforms to the equipment directly above, however, the slats are also radiused in order to create a seamless overhead terrain. The columns and wine storage, suspended from the ceiling in the middle of the hall, serve to uphold this fiction. To acknowledge the historical character of the building, the ceiling hovers away from all interior walls and instead finds its support in suspension from above. Nearly running the entire width of the space, each rib of the undulated ceiling is made from unique pieces of three-quarter-inch birch plywood assembled like pieces of a puzzle. Certain areas of the ceiling drip and slump, belying the location of exit signs, lighting features, and other details. The dining room itself was dressed in warm woods and relaminated bamboo to amplify the striping already at play throughout the interior. Striations of the ground, the furnishings, and the ceiling all conspire to create a total effect, seemingly embedding the diners in the grain of the restaurant. Despite the monumentality of the vertical construction, however, diners are never fooled: they have glimpses from their tables into the service space above – the architects have let them in on the secret.

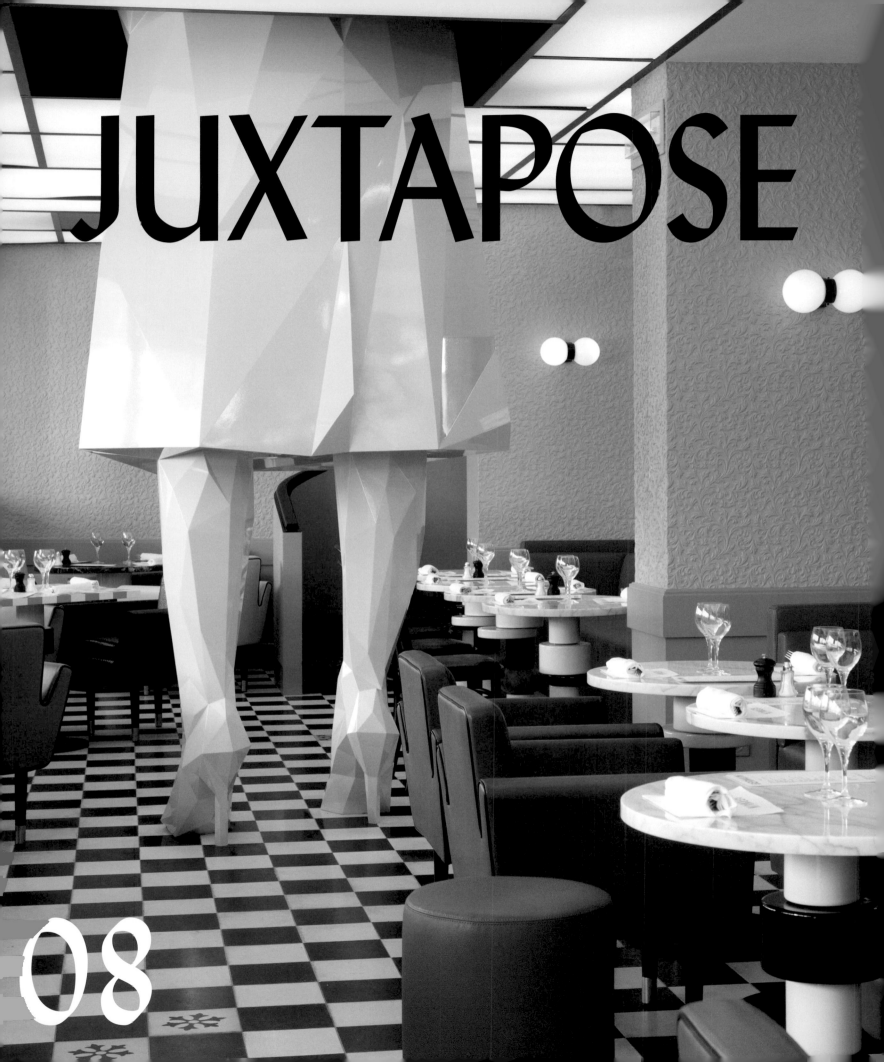

JUXTAPOSE

08

There is nothing that keeps a space as freshly engaging as contrast. By juxtaposing opposites and suggesting contradictions,

interiors keep their audience alert, awake, and sometimes even arguing. The restaurant is a stage: arranged scenographically, it becomes a locus of drama that draws diners out of their quotidian routine, into another world. And that's a good thing. Any old opposites will do: historical and modern, inside and out, private and public, red and blue, local and global, industrial and

domestic, the familiar and the strange. Diners can escape into Denis Kosutic's ORLANDO DI CASTELLI interior, which mashes together the characters of Queen Elizabeth, American rapper 50 Cent and a girl from Tyrol in a single, white room like a particularly schizophrenic stream of consciousness text scribbled euphorically on a blank piece of paper. One of Turkish design firm Autoban's café's brings Achille Castiglioni into the 18th century; another mixes steel beams and heavy glazing with homey furnishings and warm walnut wood. Copenhagen nightspot KARRIERE confuses restaurant and gallery, taking pop art and postmodern design-art off their precious white plinths and brings them into the dining room to create an eatery where consumption of culture is as natural as the consumption of food. Well, isn't it?

[•] OPEN & SHUT → p. 152

STUDIO ILSE
Matbaren, 2007, Stockholm / Sweden

Client : **Mathias Dahlgren Grand Hotel Stockholm** |
Design : **Studio Ilse (Ilse Crawford)** |
Photography : **Åke E:son Lindman**

This hotel restaurant offers two varieties of dining experience, conveniently indicated by their names: the two-starred a la carte *"Matsalen"* (The Dining Room) and the one Michelin star *"Matbaren"* (The Food Bar). Chef Mathias Dahlgren tapped creative director and designer Ilse Crawford to echo the character of his cooking, which brings traditional Swedish culture together with modern global influences. Crawford's response was a 38-guest dining room where the furnishings – like the chunkily elegant Scandinavian chairs – articulate the eating experience, which is based on the juxtaposition of creative cuisine and its traditional presentation. *Matbaren* seats 50 guests and offers a quicker but high-quality service in a more robust and natural setting, reflecting the eating experience which, contrary to *Matsalen*, revolves around the presentation of traditional cuisine in an unconventional form. The entrance bar distinguishes between these two environments by displaying an oversized, gilded narrative screen. Created by the Dutch Studio Job, culinary tools, rustic Swedish icons, and Viking ships are placed together in an intricate pattern.

BEARAND-BUNNY
Usine, 2009,
Eindhoven / the Netherlands

Amsterdam-based Bearandbunny were responsible for the overall concept, naming, logo, and interior design of this Eindhoven seafood restaurant and tearoom, which once served as a factory where the first Philips lightbulbs were manufactured. The designers took their inspiration from an old Philips Electronics poster on which the factory is pictured, surrounded by a cloud of various light bulbs, with the tagline: "Les plus grandes usines du monde." This sentence gave direction to the interior design and was later turned into the restaurant's own tagline: "Usine, le plus grand cafe du monde." On the ground floor of the historical building, Bearandbunny stitched together both factory and bistro. They first preserved the bones of the factory: the bright, mullioned windows and the extreme scale, even adding industrial touches of their own in the form of mid-century task lighting and floor-to-ceiling shelving. Then they inserted checkered black-and-white tiled café floors, a profusion of multicolored seating, and, greeting guests at the glazed entrance, a chandelier of smoked glass globes that might have come out of the nearby Design Academy.

WOODS BAGOT
AND HECKER
PHELAN &
GUTHRIE

Ivy, 2008, Sydney / Australia

Client : **Justin and Bettina Hemmes / Merivale** |
Design : **Collaboration of Woods Bagot, Hecker Phelan & Guthrie
and Merivale** | Branding and Signage : **Cornwell Studio** | Photography : **Trevor
Mein & Shannon McGrath**

Ivy is a landscaped oasis for the public within a predominantly commercial area. The interior was conceived as a green oasis containing over twenty thousand square meters of hospitality venues, including eighteen bars, nine restaurants, one of Sydney's largest ballrooms, two penthouse suites, a rooftop pool, and a "secret" sunken courtyard. Drawing inspiration from modern Los Angeles and Florida case study houses by architects such as Paul Rudolph, Richard Neutra, and John Lautner, *Ivy* recalls Palm Springs glamour and nostalgia. The interior design philosophy placed a strong focus on creating the illusion of a domestic environment through a series of interconnecting rooms, each with its own character and function. The scale of the soft furnishings and lighting – clustered in groups – alongside one-off pieces, creates an intimacy that encourages conversation, as though patrons are entertaining in their very own living rooms. A lavish rooftop pool, an internal courtyard, and a grand spiral staircase work to connect the interactive indoor/outdoor spaces, and to define the character of this playground.

JUMP STUDIOS
The Modern Pantry,
2009, London / UK

Client : **The Modern Pantry** | Photography : **Rachael Smith**

London-based architecture and design practice Jump Studios created *The Modern Pantry* for chef Anna Hansen. The two-story restaurant and shop takes up two landmarked Georgian buildings – one a townhouse, the other a former steel foundry – that were nearly derelict before the renovation. To match Hansen's homemade, folksy but modern palate, the space was rendered with an equally home-y but contemporary aesthetic. Jump sought to reconnect guests to traditional architectural references in new and intriguing ways, just as the chef was doing through her culinary practice. The historical buildings provided a sense of the traditional and the domestic while the architects provided the update: they painted chunky lathe-turned tables and simple dining room chairs white to give them a strong unity and allow them to contrast with – and pop off – the darkly stained wooden floors. They also created lampshades out of copper, almost as if the cook had simply upturned a sink load of saucepans from the nearby kitchen.

DOMESTIC ARCHITECTURE
Cupcake Royale,
2009, Seattle / USA

Client : **Cupcake Royale** | Lead Design : **Roy McMaki** |
Project Architect : **Ian Butcher** | Photography : **Mark Woods**

"Our goal was to design a space that is simultaneously familiar, friendly, new, and strange," says Domestic lead designer Roy McMakin of the studio's *Cupcake Royale* bakery. Almost impossibly, Domestic hit on a recipe for this 3000-square-foot eatery that appeals to kids, their parents, and to the hip local urbanites who want a sweet treat. The ingredients were simple opposites and avoided the saccharine: unembellished concrete floors and walls, stainless steel, and marble were paired with Amish-made chairs, maple butcher blocks, and stained glass, while soft, delicate shapes were paired with the thick sharp angles of a custom-made food display or bench.

Cremant, 2006, Seattle / USA

Client : **Cremant** | Lead Design : **Roy McMakin** | Project Architect : **Ian Butcher** | Project Manager : **Tracy Langford** | Photography : **Mark Woods**

Domestic Architecture's design of the roughly 2000-square-foot Seattle-based *Cremant* "is meant to feel like the memory or dream of a neighborhood bistro somewhere and sometime in France," says Domestic designer Roy McMakin who has also produced a chair for UK manufacturer Established & Sons. This little boîte is intended to feel familiar and unfamiliar simultaneously. Instead of explicitly recreating a small patch of France, the studio strove to create something original that would nonetheless trigger that association. Though its concrete floors, partial concrete walls, and painted wood cabinets seem ordinary enough, the odd geometry of the ceiling is emphasized charmingly by custom pale gray wallpaper and the rounded edges of the bespoke furniture – both rustic and modern – which was designed by McMakin.

ARCHITEKTUR DENIS KOSUTIC
Orlando di Castello,
2009, Vienna / Austria

Client : **Palais Gastronomie GmbH, Vienna** | Project Management : **Mareike L. Kuchenbecker** | Employees : **Carina Haberl, Judith Wölkl, Matteo Trentini** | Photography : **Lea Titz**

Kosutic's restaurant interior blends the unlikely worlds of Queen Elizabeth, the rapper 50 Cent and a girl from Tyrol in a single, predominantly white room. Delicate flowers and metallic nuts are repeated throughout the room in variations to generate powerful contrasts that somehow cohere. The proportions are unusual and everything morphs into something else: baseboards transform themselves into wallcoverings, floor lamps – suspended downwards – become ceiling lights, and benches explode into small, kidney-shaped segments that cushion the walls. White is combined with touches of metallic, silver, and cold, mirrored elements where the color feels chill; elsewhere, the whiteness glows in warm light. The use of various species of seating, another example of culture clash, serves to partition and zone the space. A tactical approach to lighting – with different shades of light targeted narrowly to different zones – create subtly different moods in each area.

|[+] OPEN & SHUT → p. 154

DESIGN RESEARCH STUDIO

Shoreditch House,
2007, London / UK

Client : **Shoreditch House** | Design : **Tom Dixon**

Design Research Studio and Tom Dixon mixed a smoothly complex cocktail in their design of the 4000-square-meter private members club, *Shoreditch House,* which takes up the top three floors of London's old Biscuit Factory. The 14 diverse interiors contain measured doses of the local vernacular, the Soho House's opulent version of a "home away from home" aesthetic, along with Dixon's own British futurist proclivities. The assignment was to translate the successful Soho House look-and-feel to suit the Shoreditch audience whilst maintaining the historic, raw qualities of the Biscuit Building. Using reclaimed and weathered materials like wood from Hastings Sea Defenses and marble from India, DRS took a natural approach to finishes, materials, and furniture. Alongside a private bowl-

ing alley named "The Biscuit Pin," a Cowshed Spa, a gym and private meeting rooms, the team concocted the Brasserie Bar with a riveting combination of copper and petrol blues and the House Kitchen, inspired by the concept of an Italian trattoria, which features 910-mm-diameter dome pendants spun from raw aluminum and hanging above refectory-style kitchen tables. They relied on views of London for wallpaper and it works.

HECKER PHELAN & GUTHRIE
Village Green Marquee,
2008, Melbourne / Australia

Client: **bttb events** | Photography: **Shannon Mc Grath**

This frivolous and cheeky temporary marquee with a view of the racing directly at Melbourne's Flemington track revisits the traditional garden party and the glamour of a trackside view of spring horse racing. Designers Hecker Phelan & Guthrie worked to pare the design down to celebrate the original spirit of the Flemington Birdcage venue, but also so that guests could experience classic racing at its most exaggerated and humorous – think Pimms on the lawn, vintage furniture, English china, strawberries and cream, British fusion tunes, and waitresses in 50s-inspired dresses serving high tea. The design team played with scale, adding oversized pots that served as the bar, too-big picket fences and a gigantic bespoke light pendant, ottomans, and waitstaff uniforms made from a gorgeously garish pink floral textile (found at Melbourne's Dancing Queen Fabrics). Underfoot in the viewing deck, a synthetic lawn was laid to help bring "the outside in" and to complete the aesthetic of white wicker lounge chairs. Living flora is a reoccurring theme in HP&G's portfolio, so real topiary trees and pot plants were added. A big plus: bttb sought to reuse as many of the interior elements as possible, including reupholstering existing furniture rather than purchasing new pieces to minimize waste, as well as using soy-based paints and recycled timbers. "I was over all the bling and superficiality," says Corina Baldwin of client events company bttb. "I wanted to concentrate on the basics."

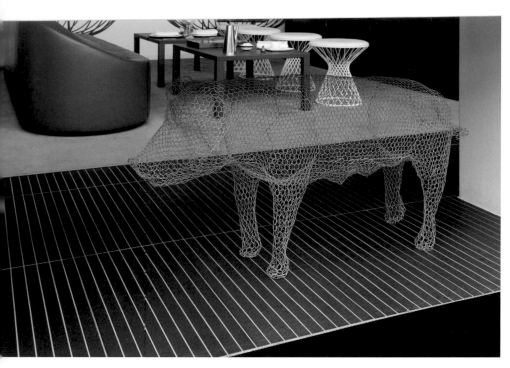

LOGICA: ARCHITETTURA

Home Delicate Restaurant,
2008, Milan / Italy

Client ⏐ **Monica Bagnari** ⏐ Design ⏐ **Riccardo Salvi & Luca Rossire** / **Logica:architettura** ⏐ Photography ⏐ **Filippo Bamberghi** ⏐ Supporting Sponsors of the Home Delicate Concept and Donators of all Furniture On-site ⏐ **AGAPE Design, EMU, DEROMA, Iris Ceramica, Seletti, Leefanders, Pieke Bergmans, Jannelli & Volpi, Mauro Bolognesi, Kose Milano, Zone Denmark, Viridea, Giacomo Benevelli (sculptor)**

Renovated by architect Riccardo Salvi and creative consultant Luca Rossire in Milan's Zona Tortona, *Home Delicate Restaurant* blurs the boundaries between private and public, inside and out. The different zones – starting at the entrance and extending into the inner garden and the living room – overlap in order to cultivate a feeling of cozy informality. A long entrance corridor plucks clients out of the city's chaos and lands them, at its end, in a secret garden. Although the furnishings will be changed out on an ongoing basis, the mood is elegant and rarefied, evoking the lightness and carelessness of the 1950s, Saint Tropez, Brigitte Bardot, and Mon Oncle's Jacques Tati.

AUTOBAN
The House Cafe Kanyon, 2009, Istanbul / Turkey
Design: **Seyhan Özdemir & Sefer Çaglar** | Photography: **Ali Bekman**

Into one of the most architecturally sophisticated mall complexes of the day, Istanbul-based Autoban inserted this interior for longtime client, *The House Café*, the franchise for whom they have already designed a subtly varied series of cafés across the city. This design is an amalgam of the mall's strikingly tiered, terraced, and canted architecture; *The House Café's* strong domestic-chic brand identity; and the Autoban aesthetic. A trapezoidal, site-built structure made of steel and glass functions as a transparent box to house the café, and fits hand-in-glove into the mall's valley-like terrain. A walnut platform forms the floor while adding warmth to the otherwise industrial frame. Although it is an architectural addition in its own right, it is widely open to the steel and glass of Kanyon's vast walls and, in this way, has a distinct identity while blending in dynamically with its surroundings.

The House Cafe Corner, 2008, Istanbul / Turkey
Design: **Seyhan Özdemir & Sefer Çaglar** | Photography: **Ali Bekman**

This *House Cafe* location combines the brand's domestic warmth with the chic cosmopolitanism of the surrounding neighborhood. Added to an historical corner in the tony Nisantasi shopping and creative district, the café actually incorporates part of the stately 18th-century Tesvikiye Mosque, preserving the original bricks of the wall and engravings on the eaves which lend texture, color, and authenticity to the space and make a rich blend with modern objects like the Castiglioni Taraxacum lamp.

SERENDIPITY3
2008, Florida / USA

The 1200-square-foot *Serendipity3* at the
Boca Raton Resort & Club is the offspring
of a legendary and eponymous midtown
Manhattan forebearer that opened in 1954
to serve an opulent menu of desserts and ice
creams, including its signature Frrrozen Hot
Chocolate, the Apricot Smush, and the world's
most expensive frozen treat (a few years ago
it was an ice cream sundae that cost $1000;
today, their $25,000 dessert is the Frrrozen
Haute Chocolate). If Serendipity3 sells candied
kitsch, the new interior magnifies the kitsch
times three. Above café tables encircled with
pink-cushioned wrought-iron ice cream parlor
chairs and plush salmon banquettes, the ceiling
is hung with a variety of stained glass pendant
lights, as if not just one but several posh parlors
were superimposed on this very sweet spot
of real estate. Somewhere inside one almost
expects to find a flask with the words "Eat Me"
printed on it. Whatever the case, customers are
swallowing it whole.

IPPOLITO FLEITZ GROUP

Bella Italia, 2007,
Stuttgart / Germany

Client: **Bella Italia Weine** | Photography: **Zooey Braun**

Wine shop as well as restaurant, *Bella Italia* was run for many years by its Sicilian owner out of an intimate living room-like space. The new, necessarily larger restaurant is located at the foot of a Wilhelmina-style residential building in Stuttgart West, an urban district popular with the city's creative class. Ippolito Fleitz strategically preserved the familial, domestic atmosphere of the original restaurant by using a profusion of ordinary but charming domestic objects: looking glasses, lathe-turned chairs, and a variety of pendant lights that might illuminate a sitting room. The character of the room is dominated by two elements: On the ceiling, the designers mounted more than 90 different gilt-framed mirrors found at rummage sales. The second element is a room within the room. This wall-less micro-architecture contains a large oval table, a round mirror, a wall sheathed in textile, a carpet, and a cluster of lamps hanging from the ceiling. All in all, the effect, with a color scheme emphasizing gray, white, and shades of lavender, is of a clean, well-lit and well-loved salon. Large shelving units with rounded corners add a strong feeling of modernity to the cozy interior while also tastefully promoting the sale of wine.

KARRIERE

2008, Copenhagen / Denmark

Art: Franz Ackermann [DE], Kristoffer Akselbo [DK], AVPD [DK], Kenneth Balfelt [DK], Bank & Rau [DK], Massimo Bartolini [ITA], Monica Bonvicini [ITA], Janet Cardiff & George Bures Miller [CAN], Maurizio Cattelan [ITA], Gardar Eide Einarsson [NO], Olafur Eliasson [DK/ISL], Michael Elmgreen & Ingar Dragset [DK/NO], Ceal Floyer [UK], FOS [DK], Alicia Framis [SPA], Dan Graham [USA], Tue Greenfort [DK], Douglas Gordon [UK], Carl Michael von Hausswolff [SE], Jeppe Hein [DK], Carsten Höller [DE], Jesper Just [DK], Ernesto Neto [BRA], Dan Peterman [USA], Tino Sehgal [UK], Tomas Saraceno [ARG], Claude El Skorra=i [INT], Robert Stadler [FRA], Simon Starling [UK], Rirk=it Tiravanija [THAI/USA], Johannes Wohnseifer [DE]

World-class installations – a hybrid of art and design objects – fill *Karriere* in the Flæsketorvet neighborhood of Copenhagen, only it is not a gallery, but a restaurant and bar. Olafur Eliasson has contributed three lights while Dan Graham's Dividing Wall, set amongst outdoor café tables, is a quandary of reflective, sheer, perforated steel and glass. Diners can listen through some panels and see through others. The Virgin Mary and Adolf Hitler (statuettes by Maurizio Cattelan) inhabit one room, while Kristoffer Akselbo's toaster tattoos the morning toast with the Mona Lisa, and Robert Stadler's puns and proverbs ornament washroom mirrors. This is a woefully partial list and it will continue to grow. The artwork that gave its name to the bar is a sign that sits at the rear of the space, by artists Michael Elmgreen and Ingar Dragset. None lesser than Ernesto Neto furnished the lounge while, nearby, in an unexpected reversal, water shoots from a drain to splash the faucet in Massimo Bartolini's industrial sink artwork called Fountain. What is art? What is design? The question is blissfully moot (and one suspects, a bit naïve) at *Karriere*.

MAURICE MENTJENS
NWE Vorst, 2007,
Tilburg / the Netherlands

Client: **NWE Vorst Theater**

The *NWE Vorst* theater in Tilburg is housed in a neo-baroque mansion, built circa 1872. Today, the building is home to a theater for contemporary drama, a ballet studio, and rehearsal rooms for young theater companies. The historic building with its grand, high-ceilinged rooms and cultural occupants inspired Mentjens to opt for a neo-modernist baroque concept in the new restaurant interior. Clustered around the light gray central entrance hall, five salons are distinguished by a unique color scheme (the three primary colors plus black and white), as was common in baroque palaces. The theater café is located in the black and white salons, the restaurant in the red salon. The black and white chambers are situated next to each other and are connected by large openings in the wall. Both rooms have an identical bar, reminiscent of an altar, with a triptych-like bottle rack. This black and white color palette conjures up a polarity between the two rooms; black and white, night and day, negative and positive. This polarity represents the dualism between quotidian reality and the illusions of nighttime dreams or the theater. Because the black salon was originally the hunt-ing room, evidenced by images of animals depicted in the plasterwork of the ceiling, Mentjens paid homage to well-known animals from literature and theater, such as Reynard the Fox, the Middle Dutch Lanceloet and the white-footed deer, and the mythical unicorn. These legendary creatures are depicted in high-gloss black on the black matt walls and ceiling, and seem to float like stars in a pitch-black sky. Red – said to stimulate the appetite – is the color of the *NWE Vorst* restaurant. The geometric pattern of red beams on the ceiling recalls a baroque garden. In the center of this upside-down garden is a large glowing globe, bathing the room in warm light.

ROBERT STADLER

Corso Trudaine and Corso Place Franz Liszt, 2007 and 2009, Paris / France

Client : **Costes Group** | Photography : © **Marc Domage**

Stadler has approached his design for the Corso restaurant chain by working to make the brand recognizable without simply repeating the same tired elements. To accomplish this, he bases each design on the bistro's site and context. Sometimes, as in *Corso Trudaine,* the restaurant will appear as a traditional bistro with a single primary furniture element that is conspicuously different from the rest of the interior, reminding diners "that this is today," says Stadler. "I see this project as a precise injection of design doses in order to achieve a functional and unpretentious restaurant with a strong identity."

The *Corso Place Franz Liszt* was the location that announced the Corso chain. There are several elements recalling the first Corso bistro on the Avenue Trudaine, but also new ones, such as the bar and tables made out of Ductal concrete, lights with reflectors made of golden sticky tape, specially cut mirrors, and shelves filled with the favorite novels of the designer's friends.

The renovated *Corso Trudaine* preserves the place's bistro-like spirit but contrasts it with some radically different and contemporary elements. The main object expressing this singular cohabitation is the coral-colored, resin-lacquered bar,

which is composed of several counter pieces melted into each other. Additional sections that seem to have their provenance in the bar but have splintered off and become embedded in other walls are projected into the rest of the space.

257

INDIA MAHDAVI
Germain, 2009, Paris / France

Client : **Thierry Costes** | Photography : **Derek Hudson**

Paris-based architect and designer India Mahdavi has built her reputation on the eclecticism of her international projects, which bring together architecture and scenography, interior, furniture, and object design. In *Germain,* as always, Mahdavi designer Apolline pieces together a comfortable though elegant atmosphere by uniting real world elements with fragments of the surreal. On ground level, a black-and-white checked five-and-dime floor is reflected and then skewed in the unusually shaped ceiling panels above. A smattering of straight-backed chairs is supplemented with slender cushy armchairs at the café tables. An artwork called Sophie, an oversized sculpture of a faceted lemon-yellow woman by Xavier Veilhan, stands on the café floor but pokes her head and torso through the ceiling into the lounge space above, in bright contrast to the blue walls of this sofa and coffee table-lined salon with its David Hicks-like carpeting.

GRAPHIC SPACES

09

The graphic restaurant interior is shaped and given its mood and personality by color or illustration. These eateries are tattooed with room-size graphics; graphics that are not simply scaled to the wall, but sometimes challenge the volume of the space, influencing the diner's perception

of its size, shape, depth or illumination. In Japan, Shinichiro Hinematsu layered thick slices of sky blue material to create every aspect of the cheerfully monolithic – and thoroughly original – VINEGAR CAFÉ. SHH Architects used industrial colors and graphics, reminiscent of road signage and construction symbols, to make a virtue of the sparseness of the APPLEMORE COLLEGE CAFETERIA. Perhaps the apotheosis of the graphic aesthetic, however, is artist Tobias Rehberger's LA BIENNALE BAR, in which he used the trompe l'oeil graphics of World War I ships – relentless stripes, triangles, and

chevrons in black, white, safety orange, and strategic doses of other colors – to dazzle visitors. In the most extreme instances, graphics give form to architecture, not the other way around.

PIERLUIGI PIU

Delicatessen Shop Olivomare,
2008, London / UK

Client: **Mr. Mauro Sanna, Oliveto & Olivo ltd.** | Structural Engineer, Planning Permissions: **Mr. Michael Blacker** | Light Consultant: **Pedro Gaiolas Pinto, of ISOMETRIX 8** | Main Contractor: **ZIBI & JACK** | Special Claddings of Toilets, Refrigerated Counter, Waiters Cabinets: **IFAS Tasselli Industria arredamenti Strada Nazionale della Cisa** | Special Seats, Claddings, Doors and Partitions: **ELEVATION Jonathan Perrot 66** | Photography: **Pierluigi Piu** (opposite page), **Giorgio Dettori** (others)

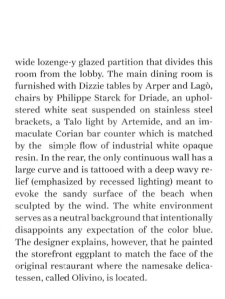

Olivomare is the last-born, belonging to the reputable London seafood brand OLIVO in the upscale Belgravia neighborhood. Piu focused on creating a formal and decorative language that would tie the new shop to its older two brethren, and make reference to the sea. He clad the wide wall that characterizes the main dining room with a highly textural pattern inspired by the works of the visionary artist Maurits Escher, in which each section of color was laser cut from a sheet of opaque laminated plastic and then juxtaposed on the vertical surface exactly as if it was a huge jigsaw puzzle. To provide a counterpoint to this, in the same room, a linear sequence of tubular luminescent "tentacles," spirals, and twists of tubular nylon mesh ("Bigoli" lampsshades by Innermost) drops down from a channel or pocket recessed in the drop-ceiling, evoking a stray shoal of jellyfish or sea anemones and the mesh of fishermen's nets, which are abstracted in a wide lozenge-y glazed partition that divides this room from the lobby. The main dining room is furnished with Dizzie tables by Arper and Lagò, chairs by Philippe Starck for Driade, an upholstered white seat suspended on stainless steel brackets, a Talo light by Artemide, and an immaculate Corian bar counter which is matched by the simple flow of industrial white opaque resin. In the rear, the only continuous wall has a large curve and is tattooed with a deep wavy relief (emphasized by recessed lighting) meant to evoke the sandy surface of the beach when sculpted by the wind. The white environment serves as a neutral background that intentionally disappoints any expectation of the color blue. The designer explains, however, that he painted the storefront eggplant to match the face of the original restaurant where the namesake delicatessen, called Olivino, is located.

LEWIS. TSURUMAKI. LEWIS ARCHITECTS
Fluff Bakery, 2004,
New York / USA

Client: **Chow Down Management** | Photography: **Michael Moran**

Lewis.Tsuramaki.Lewis's interior and storefront of bakery and coffee shop, *Fluff,* consists of a single surface made from layers of common materials. The walls and ceiling are composed of 18,500 linear feet of 3/4-inch squares of felt and stained plywood, each individually positioned and anchored in place. The mixture of gray, black, and white materials was adjusted to produce a darker area at the seats and shift to a lighter combination at ceiling height. The surface of squares generates a horizontal vertigo, drawing passersby, or at least their eyeballs, from the street through the glass storefront. As is typical of LTL, the interior surfaces, textures, and chandelier feel more akin to a gallery installation than a patisserie, always a virtue in Manhattan.

UAU STUDIO
Sosushi Take-away,
2009, Turin / Italy

Client : **Sosushi srl.** | Design : **UAU** | Architect, Project Manager : **Marco Verrando** | Photography : **Enrico Muraro** / info@enricomuraro.com

The design of this new take-out restaurant required the conversion of a former stationery store. UAU maximized the tiny space by giving each intersection of materials a use as shelves, benches, and cubbies. Clean swathes of Plexwood line the walls and are emphasized by a matte white finish while furniture details are highlighted in magenta.

SHINICHIRO HIMEMATSU

Vinegar Cafe SU,
2007, Fukuoka / Japan

Client : **Hideyuki Ooyama** | Design : **Shinichiro Himematsu**

Hinematsu renovated a 130-year-old private house to create this café and adjoining vinegar factory. The café sells the bottled vinegar, serves dishes in which the vinegar figures prominently, and even offers vinegar-sprinkled cooking lessons. The ivy-covered residential exterior was preserved in order to integrate the business into its peaceful village and agricultural surroundings where fruits like grapes, peaches, strawberries, and persimmons are raised (and used, yes, to produce vinegar). The interior, however, was radically reconstructed using the term "slice" as its theme. The space is marked by its glacial blue, horizontally layered surfaces from which the café's tables, chairs, benches, shelves, and counter are composed. The floor, walls, and ceiling have 105 mm panel joints that are laminated to form these nonetheless monolithic-feeling pieces of furniture. The effect? A cool blue interior that feels dramatically fresh.

C18
ARCHITEKTEN
Olli's Tagesbar, 2007,
Schwäbisch Hall / Germany

Client : **Oliver Jerkovic** | Photography : **Brigida Gonzales**

This 120-square-meter bar and café consists of matte white (walls, chairs, tables), glossy
black (floors), and stainless steel (fixtures, table
legs) except where there is a single, magnified
pink flower blossoming across an entire wall.
And again there, where the waiters' service areas are enclosed in tall slender glass walls that
are printed with the same tropically stirring
graphic, enlarged to the point of lyrical abstraction. The architects chose to use very few precisely placed and anchored items, opting for four
large tables and two kitchen blocks and otherwise using furnishings that can be moved at will.
The blushing effect is powerful inside but, seen
through the rough, one-meter-thick stone facade
of the medieval building in which it occupies the
ground floor, the sensation is of glimpsing fine
undergarments beneath frumpy business attire:
intriguing, to say the least.

BAUPILOTEN
Café at the Technical University, 2008, Berlin / Germany

Client : **TU Berlin** | Architecture : **Susanne Hofmann with the Baupiloten** | Project Management : **Dipl.-Ing. Martin Janekovic** **(Design), Dip. Arch. Marlen Weiser (Construction), Dipl.-Ing. Monica Wurfbaum (Consulting)** | Photography : **Jan Bitter, www.janbitter.de**

In the renovated main building of Berlin's Technical University, the Baupiloten have designed a cafeteria that connects two courtyards located within the landmarked 19th-century building while providing them with a new function. The cafeteria's distinctive luminous ceiling is visible from the university's foyer and through the windows of the inner courtyards, lined with eight tear-shaped textiles. These "ceiling drops" – the form of which is derived from gravity's mastery of the material – break the formal dominance of the room's beams. The underside of the material is constituted by a faintly transparent, white, artificial turf that not only distributes light but also regulates room acoustics. The seasons dictate the color of the drops: The warmer the outside temperature, the cooler the color. And conversely, the cooler the temperature out-

side, the warmer the color inside. In winter the lights have a warm red and orange hue that resembles fire. In summer, a vivid teal recalls a glowing sky. Meanwhile, the brightness of the lights is regulated according to the time of day, controlled by a daylight sensor. Interestingly, the lighting also influences the perceived height of the room.

SHH
ARCHITECTS
Applemore College Cafeteria,
2009, Hampshire / UK

Client : **Applemore College** | Photography : **Gareth Gardner**

SHH was commissioned to redesign the dining area of a Southampton secondary school that was fraught with complex issues: essentially a set of knocked-together spaces, it lacked cohesiveness, was unpopular with pupils, sightlines were poor, and the space was in disrepair. SHH opened a wide entrance, introduced indoor greenery and some sheltered outdoor space, blurring the lines between indoors and out, especially since dividing walls are translucent, increasing the sense of space and exposure. SHH made a virtue of the sparsity of the space, creating a semi-industrial environment featuring bright street-oriented graphics that are softened by the view of green grass from three sides. The interior has a relaxed cafeteria feel with zoned areas, some formal and some that offer low-slung, casual seating. Suspended graphic panels also have the advantage of helping to absorb noise. Materials throughout were inspired by

nature, with an invigorating yellow and green palette offset by a striking striped floor in 2-meter-wide nonslip vinyl panels. An external shipping container shelters extra seating while, outside, screened-off concrete stools, made from Milton concrete tubes and filled with concrete and aggregate, feature the familiar flashing globe of the Belisha beacon at their center.

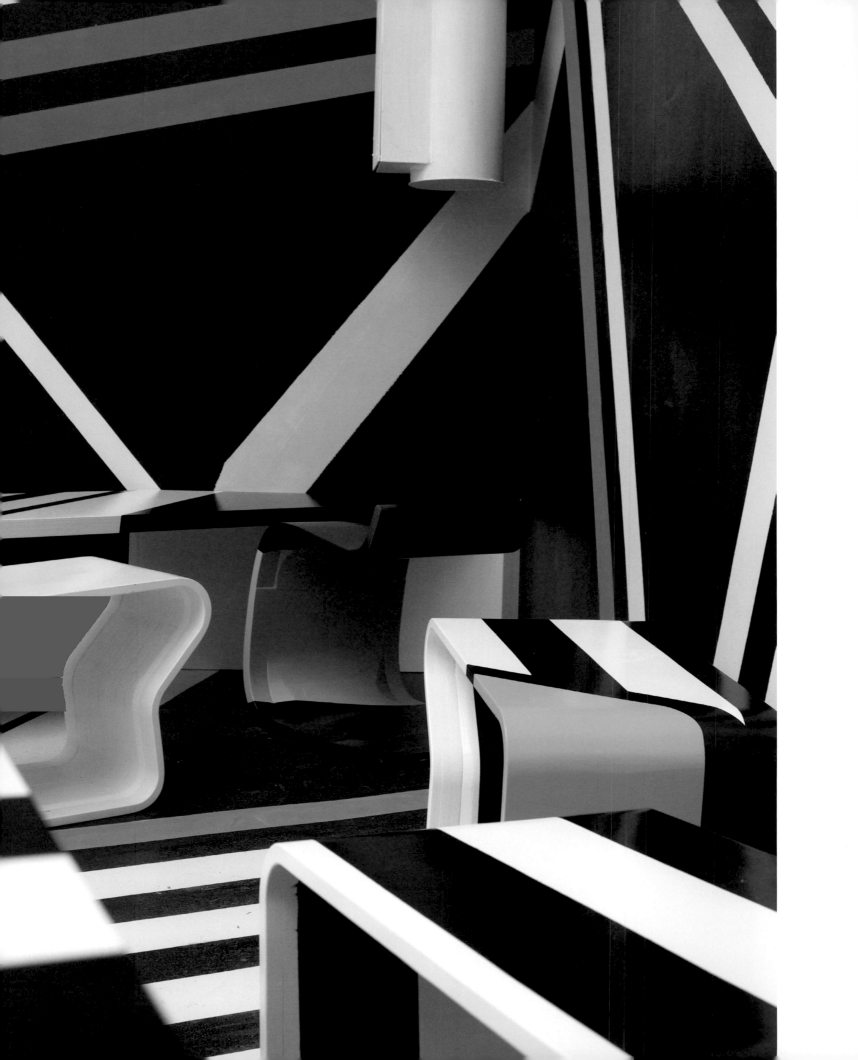

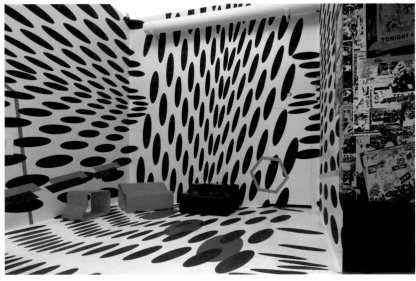

TOBIAS REHBERGER

Was du liebst, bringt dich auch zum weinen. (What you love will also make you cry), 2009, Baden-Baden / Germany and Venice / Italy

Client : **Kunsthalle Baden-Baden, Palazzo delle Esposizioni Venezia | Courtesy Neugerriemschneider, Berlin |** Photography : **Wolfgang Günzel, Images of Katja Hagelstam Courtesy of ARTEK**

During World War One, visual razzle-dazzle effects were used by the military to make it difficult for German U-boat captains to determine the position, course, and speed of ships. The Royal Navy, for one, commissioned artists to develop shimmering patterns based on cubism with which the ships were slathered. More recently, the auto industry has been using the technique to camouflage the shapes of prototypes. An 80s revival brought the effect back into design interiors, first with the successful, though temporary, razzle-dazzle pop-up Reebok shop in New York City and then with this equally extreme café by artist Tobias Rehberger (in collaboration with Finnish manufacturer Artek). Rehberger recalled the form in order to design the café / bar at the former Italian pavilion. Now dubbed "La Biennale," it earned Rehberger a Golden Lion for best artist and has become a permanent feature of the pavilion. *"What you love..."* is a febrile, acid-dropping clash of black and white stripes, mirrors, and eye-trumping patterns that confound architecture, utilities, and furnishings; disorienting users in a way that feels enchanted.

TDC

Frame Bar, 2008, Athens / Greece

Client : **St. George Lycabettus Hotel** |
Construction Management : **TDC** | Architectural Design : **Dimitrios Tsigos** |
Construction Managing Architect : **John Tsigos**

In the upscale district of Kolonaki, the *Frame* lounge's seamless modernity was imagined by architect Dimitris Tsigos, who draped ribbons of white, heat-formed Staron over delicious brown Spanish emperador marble. Tsigos began with an old book of anthropometrics and mapped typical activities that might take place in a bar and mezzanine-level restaurant: sitting, dancing, eating, talking, reclining. Using 3D Studio Max and Rhinoceros software, he smoothed seamed pieces of this "map" into continuous surfaces, allowing their shapes to morph into one another, generating what Tsigos calls "poly-surfaces." The Staron ribbons form surfaces with many functions: stairs, sinks, bar counters, café tables, some seating, partitions, floors, walls, and a DJ booth. In the restaurant, an epic throne chair peels down to become part of the floor and then peels upward again to become a table. And for those who want the relief of seeing a few seams, a large heat-formed and molded Plexiglas chandelier consists of widely sliced strips through which light pours generously over the melted landscape below.

PURESANG
Grey Goose Bar, 2008,
Brussels / Belgium

Client : **Grey Goose (Headquarters Bacardi-Martini Brussels)** |
Photography : **Frank Gielen**

When Grey Goose commissioned Puresang to design a full bar in their headquarters, the result was a rich play of blue mirrors, cut into triangles and mounted in layers
against the wall to create more depth and tactility in what was rather a small space. When the
client asked for a high-roller drinking environment that could also be used, on the opposite end
of the spectrum, as a meeting room, Puresang
simply extended the tall ribbon-like bar into a
more sober conference table, hemmed around
with Konstantin Grcic chairs. The designers also
custom-made a delicate LED chandelier for the
space, which is reflected like shards of ice in the
blue mirror. The wall at the end of the bar –
screened with illuminated Grey Goose bottles
that form a bright wall of ice – gives the room a
dramatic feeling without being too heavy-hand-
ed in its product placement role. Light and projections of light are as important to the interior
as the furniture and finishes because they create
radically different perspectives depending on
where visitors move in the space.

OUTLINE PROJECTS
Bangalore Express,
2008, London / UK

Client : **Waterloo Leisure** | Design : **Outline / Michael Westthorp**

The client commissioned a re-invention of the traditional curry house to match their vision of fast, healthy Indian food. Outline's product is an engaging space with a keen urban edge and a clever method for creating more table space. Tubular steel furniture complements the bunk bed-like double-height booths, which provide 24 extra covers over the same floor space. The booths run the length of one side of the restaurant and can be accessed by a scaffold tube step-ladder. (A mock-up of this arrangement was constructed on-site so that the designers could work out how the waitstaff would serve to this "second story" of clientele.) The space's wall cladding has a linear pattern cut into it that was done using a circular saw to make shallow grooves in the board. The cladding was then painted one solid color, after which some of the shapes – generated by the grooves – were painted in a strict palette of three contrasting colors. This generated a composition of shapes and color that draws the customer's eyes through the space in a controlled way. Outline selected two shades of green and two shades of gray to give the scheme its pop. The studio's inspiration for this wall surface came from looking at the waste board that building contractors put under sheet materials when cutting through them, a process that leaves a series of random, shallow grooves in the board beneath.

FRANKENSTEIN
Restaurant Pontus!, 2007,
Stockholm / Sweden

Client : **Pontus Frithiof and Sven Hagströmer** | Concept and Contents :
Pontus Frithiof and Pontus Frankenstein | Creative Director : **Pontus Frankenstein** | Architect : **Frankenstein Stockholm and Strategisk Arkitektur** | Furnishing and Decoration : **Frankenstein Stockholm and Agneta Pettersson / SA**

Pontus!, third in a series of Swedish dining establishments brought to life by Pontus Frithiof, folds three concepts into a three-floor Stockholm eatery: oyster and champagne bar; cocktail bar where guests can snack on dim sum, sashimi, and sushi; and a dining room serving modern, seasonal foods with a profusion of options for vegetarians. There are also DJs, sake and tea menus, and shizu martinis. Instead of starters and main courses, dishes come in three sizes so that diners can construct their meals as they see fit. This culinary whimsy is matched by an unusual décor designed by creative agency Frankenstein Stockholm: looming above more conventional and staidly elegant round booths and café tables buttoned-up in crisp white linen, the walls of the main dining room are lined with a bespoke wallpaper that depicts a vast, crowded library filled with many of the owner's favorite books – including, of course, his own: *Pontus by the Book.*

INDEX

A–D

R – W

EAT OUT

RESTAURANT DESIGN AND FOOD EXPERIENCES

Edited by ROBERT KLANTEN, SVEN EHMANN
& SHONQUIS MORENO
Text and preface by SHONQUIS MORENO

Cover by FLOYD SCHULZE for Gestalten
Cover Photography by TJEP.
Layout by FLOYD SCHULZE for Gestalten
Typefaces: Farnham by CHRISTIAN SCHWARTZ,
Foundry: www.myfonts.com
Lisbon, Foundry: www.fonts.com
Client Mono by OLOF LINDQVIST & SEBASTIAN WADSTED,
Foundry: www.gestalten.com/fonts

Project Management by JULIAN SORGE for Gestalten
Production Management by MARTIN BRETSCHNEIDER for Gestalten
Proofreading by PATRICIA GOREN
Printed by SIA Livonia Print, Riga
Made in Europe

Published by Gestalten, Berlin 2010
ISBN 978-3-89955-254-6

Bibliographic information published by the Deutsche
Nationalbibliothek.
The Deutsche Nationalbibliothek lists this publication
in the Deutsche Nationalbibliografie;
detailed bibliographic data is available on the
internet at http://dnb.d-nb.de.

This book was printed according to the internationally
accepted FSC standards for environmental protection,
which specify requirements for an environmental
management system.

FSC Mixed Sources
Product group from well-managed
forests and other controlled sources
www.fsc.org Cert no. SW-COC-002883
© 1996 Forest Stewardship Council

Gestalten is a climate neutral company and so are our
products. We collaborate with the non-profit carbon
offset provider myclimate (www.myclimate.org) to
neutralize the company's carbon footprint produced
through our worldwide business activities by investing
in projects that reduce CO_2 emissions (www.gestalten.
com/myclimate).

myclimate
Protect our planet

EAT OUT

RESTAURANT DESIGN AND FOOD EXPERIENCES